RYTAN, Thank you so very much for your great referral of "DaTAl David enjoy my Book "A Bum Deal" And Always make a difference to the less fortunate. your an awesome Physical Therapist.

A BUM DEAL

An UNLIKELY JOURNEY
from HOPELESS *to* HUMANITARIAN

RUFUS HANNAH & BARRY M. SOPER

S sourcebooks

This book is a memoir. It reflects the authors' present recollections of their experiences. Some names and events have been compressed, and some dialogue has been re-created.

Published by Sourcebooks, Inc.
P.O. Box 4410, Naperville, Illinois 60567-4410
(630) 961-3900
Fax: (630) 961-2168
www.sourcebooks.com

Library of Congress Cataloging-in-Publication Data

Hannah, Rufus.
 Bum deal : an unlikely journey from hopeless to humanitarian / by
Rufus Hannah and Barry M. Soper.
   p. cm.
 1. Soper, Barry M. 2. Philanthropists--United States--Biography. 3.
Alcoholics--United States--Biography. 4. Southern States--Social
conditions. I. Soper, Barry M. II. Title.
 HV28.S66H36 2010
 361.7'4092--dc22
 [B]
                              2010026432

Printed and bound in the United States of America.
SB 10 9 8 7 6 5 4 3 2 1

Rufus Hannah dedicates this book to all the
men, women, and children who are homeless.
"May you find your way home safely."

Barry Soper dedicates this book to Ed Bradley, a
great journalist, who said that Rufus's story must be told
and that he was the one to write it. "When I told him that
I wasn't sure I could do this, he turned to me with a twinkle
in his eye and said, 'Oh yes, you really can.'"

ACKNOWLEDGMENTS

RUFUS HANNAH WISHES TO ACKNOWLEDGE HIS BEST friend, Donnie Brennan. May he be safe. Many thanks to Alcohol and Drug Treatment Program (ADTP) at the VA Hospital in La Jolla, CA. Thanks to Al Pavich, CEO at Veterans Village San Diego (VVSD); Darcy Pavich, Stand Down Coordinator; Marilyn Cornell at VVSD; Jim Mooney (also at VVSD), who always had my back; Aunt Dorothy Woods, who shared her family photo album; Michael Stoops, National Coalition for the Homeless, for allowing me to participate and make a difference with his organization's Faces of Homelessness Speaker's Bureau; Professor Brian Levin, Cal State San Bernardino, who recommended me for the Civil Rights award from the California Association of Human Relations Organizations (CAHRO); Greg Kyritsis of the California Police Officers Standards Training (POST) in allowing Barry and me to being involved in the making of the training film regarding the way officers treat the homeless.

And, of course, great thanks to Barry Soper, for so many reasons.

Barry Soper wishes to acknowledge Jill Marsal of the Marsal Lyon Literary Agency, who gave this unknown writer's manuscript a chance to find a home; the truly amazing editor, Peter Lynch and the staff at Sourcebooks, whose exceptional comments and vision made this book come alive; Mike Sirota, my writing coach and friend, who kept me in the ball game; Dick Carlson in Washington, D.C., my closest friend, whose advice and support were critical at the various stages of the writing; Michael Karzis of CBS News's *60 Minutes*, a special thank you for allowing me ten precious minutes alone with the legend, Ed Bradley, and the professionalism and caring you showed Rufus and Donnie; the late actress Carrie Snodgress for her compassion and caring toward Rufus and Donnie; Sandy Burgin of MLB.com; screenwriter Scott Silver; Paul Krueger, NBC News; Bill Ritter, ABC News New York; Dave Balsinger of Grizzly Adams Productions; Christine Whitmarsh; Phyllis Ullman; photojournalist Susan Madden Lankford; photographer Alice Gerschler; public relations specialist Kathy Pinckert: George Mitrovich of the City Club of San Diego for allowing me to listen and meet the great writers whom he brings to San Diego; Donnie's mother, Virginia Brennan, a saint, for the use of the photo album and the background on Donnie and Rufus; Deputy District Attorney Curtis Ross and detective Dan Willis for their roles in the prosecution of the *Bumfights* case. A special thank you to civil litigators Browne Greene and Mark Quigley for representing Rufus and Donnie in the civil case and helping them get their dignity back; Bonnie Dumanis, District Attorney, San Diego; State Senator Darrell Steinberg for his help with SB122 Hate Crime legislation to protect the homeless. Additional thanks to cousin Adam and Cara Goucher, who taught me that it's not how you start the race but how you finish it; my parents in heaven, who taught my brother Robert and I by example to always help the less fortunate; my cousin Barry Plotkin, for being part of the adventure; my sons Blair and Josh and daughter, Jill, for their love and support in making a difference in a person's life.

And, of course, many thanks to Rufus Hannah, the most courageous person I have ever had the privilege to know.

PREFACE

AUTHORS' NOTE

BARRY SOPER: IN 2006, SHORTLY BEFORE HIS DEATH, ED Bradley of *60 Minutes* interviewed Rufus Hannah and Donnie Brennan regarding their roles in the infamous *Bumfights* videos in particular, and about violence against homeless people in general. When I spoke to Mr. Bradley afterward, he acknowledged my part in helping Rufus and Donnie "escape" from the young filmmakers who had taken advantage of them for years and in guiding them through the legal process to make sure their voices were heard. Mr. Bradley suggested that I write a book about my experiences. I told him that I hadn't thought about writing a book, but it seemed like a great idea.

Rufus Hannah: I didn't trust Barry—I hardly ever trusted anyone back then—when he was helping us out after we were done with *Bumfights*. But after I began my recovery from forty years of alcoholism—Barry helped me through that too—I came to realize that this man had a huge heart. I began to open up, telling him not only what had happened during the time we were making the *Bumfights* videos, but also about my life all the way back to a small town in Georgia. I told him things that I never told another soul, and it felt good to get it all out.

Barry Soper: Hearing Rufus's life story stunned me. It made his "comeback" even more amazing and inspiring. I decided that just telling the *Bumfights* part of his life was not enough, so with his permission I wrote it all down. *A Bum Deal: An Unlikely Journey From Hopeless to Humanitarian* is presented in Rufus Hannah's voice—as it should be.

INTRODUCTION

JANUARY 7, 2008

HEAVY RAINS AND WIND HAD CLOBBERED THE CAPITAL city of Sacramento for the past week. And if that wasn't bad enough, I was late—really late. I looked away from the flashing lights tracking the elevator's progress and checked my watch. I glanced back up at the floor numbers and in doing so got a look at my reflection in the fancy mirror overhead. For a moment, I hardly recognized the neatly groomed guy named Rufus Hannah looking back at me. I offered a little prayer to God, asking for the strength to use my voice to speak for so many others who didn't have one—and, of course, for guiding me out of the darkness and back into the light.

The elevator arrived at the right floor and I got out. As I rushed down the hall toward the main ballroom of the Embassy Suites, I couldn't help but notice how hard the rain pounded against the windows overlooking the city. I felt real lucky to be inside on a rain-soaked, chilly day like this instead of out on the streets, trying like mad to find shelter from the harsh weather. Back when I was homeless, these days were the worst. It was bad enough already, crawling like a rat through Dumpsters, trying to find food or anything that resembled it. But when the weather was awful, life was unbearable and full of despair on every street corner. Nowhere to hide, no way to ever really feel warm, fed, or rested. All you could do was keep walking, keep moving, and hope that things got better.

I stepped away from the hotel windows, approached the entrance of the ballroom, and looked in. Hundreds of well-dressed people milled around, shaking hands and talking among themselves. Someone pointed me in the direction of my table near the front of the large, elegantly decorated room. As I made my way through the crowd, some people rushed forward to shake my hand and congratulate me on my "remarkable achievement." They thanked me for wanting to speak on behalf of those who had no voice. Didn't they know how I used to be one of those same people? They kind of forgot that, looking at me now, all cleaned up.

"Rufus, thank God. What are you trying to do, give us a heart attack?" one of my friends exclaimed. Brian Levin, a Stanford Law School alumnus and national expert on homelessness, motioned for me to sit down. He looked frantic that I was late. I suddenly felt bad about my lifelong habit of always getting into trouble and setting people off, even though most of the time I didn't mean it.

I sat in my seat, picked up the event program, and started reading it. There I was, on the prestigious list of civil rights award recipients: *Rufus Hannah.* The program talked about how I "overcame embarrassment, unemployment, alcoholism, and disabilities to turn his life around and in the process help others." Was this me? Heck, I felt like I was reading about someone else.

I picked up a pen and started jotting down some notes on the back of the program. I was supposed to give a speech when I got the award, but I had no idea what to say. Given what my life had been like in recent years, I felt as if this were some kind of bad dream. How do you sum up a whole life in a couple of minutes—especially one that started in such a distant place from where it was now? I thought about being born in a small Southern town, beginning my life by drinking beer from a baby bottle, getting kicked out of school, the whole army disaster, the crazy van trip out West, train jumping—and then, all those years I spent as a homeless drunk.

And, of course, the *Bumfights* videos—when I risked life and limb for booze while some kids filmed the whole damn thing. Looking at all this on paper, I wondered how any man could have survived. I wondered how my body *did* survive, especially with all the alcohol I drank.

I flipped the program over to see if there were any hints about what I was supposed to say. It mentioned things about the history of the civil rights award they'd be giving me. When I saw the words *civil rights* I instantly thought of great men like Martin Luther King Jr. and John F. Kennedy—certainly not me.

As I continued reading through the program, marveling over the impressive list of recipients and their accomplishments—wondering how in the heck I was even in the same room with them, let alone on the same list—I noticed my hands. They were cracked and calloused from my work as a painter and handyman, but that wasn't what I was looking at. Even after a number of painful and expensive laser treatments, the letters were still there, tattooed across my knuckles: B-U-M-F-I-G-H-T. I thought about the damage these hands had done—to me and, even worse, to my best friend…

FEBRUARY 2001

Crack! My tattooed, bloodied, filthy knuckles slammed viciously into Donnie's jaw, showing no mercy. The attack was a blind side, pure and simple, and Donnie immediately fell to the ground, instinctively throwing his hands up in the air in an attempt to protect himself. I continued to pummel my best friend, even kicking him while he was down. I vaguely heard the sound of bones cracking in one of Donnie's ankles from the force of my kicks. I caught glimpses of the black-and-blue bruises I was causing and the blood oozing from Donnie's wounds as the blows tore through swollen skin. But I continued the savage attack, too damned drunk to even realize what I was doing.

Next to us, the teenagers filming the attack whooped and hollered in triumph. This was exactly the result they had been hoping for. I swayed drunkenly, barely noticing that Donnie now cowered on the ground, whimpering, crying out in agony, and begging—*begging*—for someone to call 911. I stopped swinging and stared blankly at my now-crippled best friend, writhing on the ground in pain, and I saw what I had done. Some tears fell down my cheek.

"You know, Ryan, I don't think Rufus is MAN enough to throw the first punch!" Zachary Bubeck, one of the filmmakers, had called out. It had only been a few minutes earlier when the idea of beating the crap out of Donnie, which the kids had suggested, had sounded like the dumbest idea in the world.

"Yeah, I think he's afraid Donnie will whip his ass!" Ryan McPherson, the kingpin of the group, had replied.

We'd all gathered in a dirt lot behind a former Taco Bell restaurant in La Mesa, California, a nice suburb of San Diego. The kids were shouting excitedly at us—two middle-aged homeless dudes who were so drunk that remaining upright was a challenge. Two homeless guys: me, Rufus Hannah, age forty-eight, and Donnie Brennan, age fifty-three, my best friend of about ten years. Both veterans, we met and became friends while homeless.

I was just a little guy, and I had an overgrown gray beard that seemed to be an extension of an unruly mop of tangled grayish black hair that flew around my face. Donnie was taller than me, a chatty guy with lots of charisma who had straight, long gray hair flattened under a trucker's cap. And I couldn't understand why they thought we would fight each other.

When I was drunk, like now, people could barely understand what the heck I was saying. And when they did, my thick Southern drawl complicated things even more. "Whaddya guys want from me? Why're ya doin' this?" I remember slurring at them.

"I don't think Donnie's playing along," Ryan said. "He's not a team player, and I think he's going to ruin the project for all of us, and you're not going to make your share of the money, Rufus."

"What do I care about the money?" I snapped.

Bubeck laughed. "No money, no beer."

The monster inside my gut that needed alcohol like a fish needed water roared at me. It warned me that these punks were right—I *needed* the beer that they were taunting me with, holding over my head. I needed it *bad*. I'd already downed many more like it so far today, but I knew that those would eventually wear off and my body would hurt like hell from withdrawal if I didn't have another one.

The kids continued to goad me, trying to get me to throw the first punch so they could capture it on camera.

"Donnie isn't one of us like you are, Rufus," Ryan carried on, trying to get me to further hurt Donnie. "He's messing up the film. He's not cool like us."

But I didn't care about any of that. All I saw in my mind were the painful sweats, tremors, and muscle aches I would experience within hours if I didn't get that goddamned beer.

So I turned my mind off and laid into Donnie, landing punch after drunken punch—hard. I beat the holy hell out of the closest friend I had ever known. I punched, kicked, and slapped the one guy who had never let me down.

When the dust cleared, Donnie's leg was shattered. He would need a stainless steel rod implanted just to hold his ankle and leg together. This one thing, started by others but carried out by me, would permanently disable Donnie and eat away at my soul one teardrop at a time for years to come.

Both of us wound up bloody, bruised, and beaten—only shells of the men we once were. As an ambulance took Donnie away, I realized that we had become animals, trained to humiliate ourselves and self-destruct on the command, "Action!" just like that Pavlov guy's dog. I vaguely recalled some of the things I had done that brought me to this time and place. But it all seemed to happen so fast, like an out-of-control car speeding toward a cliff. Trouble was, when I fished around for the brake pedal, I realized that I was sitting in the backseat.

JANUARY 7, 2008

I shook my head thinking back on that day and so many others like it. *Bumfights,* the damn *Bumfights*…But it was hardly the start of my troubles. No, that began with the drinking, and it continued with estrangement from a loving family…which finally led to homelessness.

PART 1

BORN *on the* BOTTLE

CHAPTER 1
The SUNNY SIDE *of* LIFE

SOME KIDS ARE BORN WITH SILVER SPOONS IN THEIR mouths. I was born with a beer bottle in mine.

Hometown: tiny Swainsboro, Georgia. Date of birth: November 27, 1954. Rufus Jr. is what they called me, and I joined my parents, Lucille and Rufus Sr., an older sister, Jenny, and eventually a younger brother, Billy, in a mostly normal, cheerful tale of a family growing up in the Old South. My family tale included sprawling country houses and tire swings, along with more compact suburban homes. Born and raised Baptist, I have few recollections of going to church on a regular basis. When we did attend, I got stuck wearing Sunday pants, a white shirt, and a bow tie. I always felt relieved that my folks were not regular churchgoers.

True to the era, we kids spent more time outside causing mischief than cramped inside, glued to technology. The tale was complete with a 1956 bronze and white Buick and a dog named Rex. This was the sunny side of life as I grew up.

Unfortunately, there are two sides to every story.

"Dang, Lu, don't this kid ever stop his wailin'?" my dad would say as my mom struggled with me, a fussy infant.

Mom would reach for the half-consumed bottle of beer that stood on a coffee table. "Don't fret. I got an idea," she would say and then unscrew the cap of my baby bottle.

My parents, both alcoholics, would add beer to my baby bottle to keep me quiet. I found that out from my mother many years later. But even before then, when I was still in my mother's womb, the alcohol-induced damage was already in progress. However, this was not evident until the moment I was born. After the final push, Mom looked at the nurse's face and knew something was wrong. My cry was weak, and the doctor kept his eyes down as he clamped and cut the cord.

"What is it? Is he okay?" Mom demanded anxiously.

"Your son is premature and jaundiced," the doctor said as he placed the wrapped bundle on her stomach.

Although the new mom barely knew what these words meant, she did know this: the miniature sickly baby with greenish, yellow-tinted skin staring up helplessly at her was not the perfect new life that all mothers envision when they first find out they are pregnant. This precious new baby—me—they had waited so long for was not only imperfect, his life was also in grave danger.

"Hush, little one. Now you hush," Lucille Hannah whispered to me.

But as she leaned down to plant a gentle kiss on my forehead, the nurse took me away from her. Mom started to weep. "Please don't take him!" she begged.

"I'm sorry, but we need to start working on him," the nurse explained quickly, placing me in a bassinet and wheeling it out of the room.

"I did this to my baby!" my mom cried. "I damaged him. He's weak and he's gonna die because of me! How can I live with that?"

I had been born flawed, and it would take some work to fix me. I'd need two blood transfusions just to survive. As the fresh, clean blood flowed into me, an oxygen mask covering most of my tiny face, my folks stood silently by my side, praying.

"Please God, don't take our boy," my dad intoned. "Don't take 'im."

Day after day, night after night they watched, wept, and prayed. Much to their relief, I survived. So you had to wonder why they would soon be putting booze in my baby bottle.

Naturally, I wouldn't be aware of my dramatic entrance into the world, and the fact that addiction was literally in my blood, till years later. The first hints would show up as a teenager, when I felt a powerful urge to start drinking out of a whole new kind of bottle and couldn't stop.

— —

In addition to such somber childhood firsts, I also experienced more typical chronological landmarks: rented ones. My family moved a lot. I later learned that many of the moves had to do with my dad finding work, mostly as a mechanic in various industries. But as a little kid, the frequent moves confused me. My folks, Mom's sister Dorothy, Dad's brother Melvin, me, Jenny, and Bill moved as a group from street to street, neighborhood to neighborhood, town to town, and state to state, like a traveling family circus.

"Yep, we're movin' again," I would have to tell one or another short-lived friend. "Dunno where this time. My pa got a new job."

Those homes in Georgia, Tennessee, North Carolina, and even Ohio for a spell served as anchor points for my childhood memories. I remembered most of them in great detail, the pictures leaping off the pages of a long-misplaced photo album.

There was this first house, where I lived as a toddler and young boy, a small wooden house within the town limits. In Swainsboro you lived in or outside the town limits, determining the proximity of other neighbors, businesses, and life in general. My fondest memory attached to this home was of my grandmother living across the street.

Our next home was in Wadesboro, North Carolina. I was nine years old in 1963, the year of segregation battles and Martin Luther King Jr.'s "I have a dream" speech in Washington. None of us knew much about things like that. Sure, there were "coloreds" in Wadesboro, but I didn't think much about that either.

The first I heard of any historical event happening outside my nice world was one day in school. In the middle of a real boring grammar lesson, Mrs. Ratliffe was summoned into the hallway by the principal. When she came back, she told my class, "Children, I have some bad news. President Kennedy has just been killed."

"Who the hell is that?" I whispered to a classmate.

"Damned if I know," the kid whispered back.

Across the aisle, another kid laughed. "'Bout time someone shot the Yankee!" he yelled, setting off lots of relieved laughter from others in the class who apparently knew who the hell this Kennedy fellow was.

"Why? What'd he do?" I asked.

"He's a nigger lover," the kid said.

Home in Wadesboro, where a country boy like me lived when city-boy Kennedy was shot, was a towering white house next to a four-lane highway. Up until then, my mom had been a homemaker. But now we were a two-income household. My dad worked as a mechanic at a cotton mill, repairing and maintaining the weaving machines. Mom worked part-time at the same mill, sewing T-shirts.

Cotton was a big deal to our family back then. When I was two or maybe three, my hair was so white that people called me "Cotton." Around the same time, my pa worked as a cotton sharecropper.

Our family home back then was another old wooden house where water was drawn from a well in the front yard. I remember my dad taking me out to the cotton field, where I would see my grandma and the "colored" workers toiling side by side. I would lie down on the fluffy sheets of cotton, nature's most luxurious bed, for afternoon naps. I'd stuff a pillowcase with cotton that my grandma had dropped on the ground, and I'd let the warm rays of sunshine cover me up, just like a blanket.

While kids in other American homes may have been gathered around a television with their families, watching events like the Kennedy assassination, the March on Washington, and King's speech with fear, confusion, and proper awe, my siblings and I were more likely to be found outside playing. When I was nine, my outdoor activities were a bit more mischievous than lazy afternoon naps in the cotton. I would usually be dressed in blue jeans, short-sleeved, button-down checkered cotton shirts, and scuffed tennis shoes. My hair was short, not quite military, although my dad had a habit of nearly shaving Bill's and my heads in the summertime. I couldn't get my clothes worn and dirty fast enough.

I liked hunting, fishing, playing on the tire swings, climbing trees, and fixing and riding bicycles. Usually I didn't get along with Bill. He was a tattletale—always getting me in trouble. But it was real exciting when we finally got our own bikes. I was eleven then, and we had freedom.

We soon decided to take that freedom to the next level. When I was around thirteen, Bill and I took up another, less innocent hobby:

smoking. Our house stood near a path that cut through a pine thicket. We built a makeshift hut out of pine limbs and straw and then sneaked out to our secret camp and smoked cigarettes.

One unfortunate day our pa followed us and discovered the secret smoking hut. Rather than busting us right away, he bided his time, crouching outside the pine-and-straw hut, silently spying on us, not saying a word.

That night at supper, he confronted us. "Have you boys been smoking?" he demanded.

"No, Dad," Bill said, kicking me under the table just in case.

"No," I agreed.

But he already knew. Pa made it very clear that the whipping we received that night was for lying, not smoking. I learned a valuable lesson that day.

Another good ol' Southern family virtue that my dad eventually passed on to me was that a solid work ethic is an essential foundation for a productive life. From a laundry list of daily chores to joining our parents at working at our own jobs when required, we Hannah kids learned to pull our own weight at an early age. At one point Jenny worked full-time alongside our mom, sewing T-shirts at the cotton mill. Whenever something needed to be done, we were expected to help. Ours was a family that worked together, played together, and stuck together, no matter what.

My siblings and I also had another grandmother of sorts: a "colored" woman who was the family's closest neighbor, about half a mile down the road. Bill and I would visit to play basketball with her grandsons.

She was the matriarch of her family, but that's not how she was best known. This grandma was into black magic. She had a black kettle, which she used to make soap and lye, that sat in the middle of a fire pit.

"Uh-uh, she ain't making soap here," I used to tell my siblings. "Heck, this looks more like the kind of pot used by witches to brew up magical potions!"

"Rufus, you've been watching too many scary movies," Jenny chided.

Even so, I frequently visited with the fascinating old woman. I never quite knew what to expect or what she might say.

"Rufus, if you puts a live black cat in de steaming black kettle and de cat's bones come to de top, de devil will appear," she would tell me.

I would just stare up at her, thanking God that I wasn't a black cat. "Then what happens?" I would whisper.

"Den you can make any wish, and it will come true, but de devil will own your soul in exchange."

I decided right then and there to make sure never to visit this lady on Halloween.

——

I would experience many more homes, mostly in the same or nearby towns, before I turned eighteen and finally left home for good. While living in one of those homes, I experienced the first tough story of my childhood. When I was around thirteen, our family lived way out in the country in a place called Deep Creek. This home was a big plantation-style house on a farm loaded with fig, pear, and plum trees. I had recently inherited a German shepherd puppy from Aunt Dorothy, which I named Rex.

Rex and I would regularly go hunting in the woods, just like millions of other boys and their dogs. But Rex only seemed to show love and loyalty to me, not allowing anyone else to feed him.

Mom considered Rex a danger. It soon got to the point where I had to keep Rex chained up whenever we weren't together. Local kids would throw rocks at Rex, and he tried to bite them in return.

"Stupid dog!" one kid yelled.

"Why don't you act like a normal dog?" another one cried out, aiming a stone at Rex's mouth to shut him up.

When I saw the drama unfolding from my bedroom window, I ran out, toting my shotgun.

"Get outta here before I make you get outta here!" I yelled as they scattered.

"Aw, yer as crazy as that mutt!" one of them called over his shoulder.

Standing there on the front lawn with the kids sprinting down the dirt road and Rex still barking and pawing wildly, I knew it was time to make a decision.

As heartbreaking as it was, one day I took Rex off his chain to go hunting. As usual, I let him run free through the woods, frolicking and chasing after squirrels.

"Good-bye, pal," I murmured as the dog disappeared beyond a thicket. "I can't take you home no more." I wiped a tear and hurried off.

Mom was just finishing up dinner as I came in through the screen door, the gun slung over my shoulder. I had nearly made it through the kitchen before she said, "You left him?"

"Yeah."

One word was all I could choke out.

That wasn't my last hunting story without a happy ending. I wasn't actually involved in the next one, but my life would be forever changed because of it.

I went hunting a lot with my dad, using a 20-gauge pump shotgun that Pa had given me. One day, when I was a young teen, I was supposed to go hunting with my dad. But when the day came, I felt more like hanging out with my girlfriend instead and told my dad I'd decided not to go with him. So my dad took Bill and a neighborhood kid named Chris, whose father was a minister. Bill brought his .410 shotgun and Pa his .22 Springfield rifle. I loaned Chris my shotgun for the trip.

"You'll take good care of her, right?" I told Chris earlier as the group packed up their gear.

"Sure thing," Chris said.

"Kill one for me," I told Bill before heading out.

"Yeah, we'll make sure we do that," Bill replied.

Later that day, while I was at my girlfriend's house, I watched curiously as my uncle pulled up outside. My uncle grabbed me and shoved me into the backseat of the car. His face was as white as a sheet.

"What's going on? Where's Dad?" I asked.

"We'll meet him at home later on," my uncle said.

His expression made me stop wanting to ask questions. I went cold inside but didn't know why. My uncle finally revealed the disturbing details of the hunting trip turned tragedy.

"Your pa, he…he accidentally shot young Chris," he managed to gasp out. "He drove the boy to the hospital, but…Chris was dead when they got there!"

Now I went pale. My mind was still trying to sort through what my uncle had just said, but everything felt like it was in slow motion, so my brain wasn't working right.

"Your dad's at home. He ain't doing so well," my uncle added.

I continued to stare at the man in disbelief as we pulled into the driveway. Bill appeared at the front door. He seemed surprised to see us all there.

"Billy, what happened?" I asked like an idiot, as if the story would change.

It was almost as if Bill hadn't heard me. "I gotta go talk to Chris's parents," he said, looking through me like I was a ghost.

"Want me to go with you?" I asked.

I didn't really know why I asked that; it just sort of came out. This didn't seem to be the kind of news anyone should have to deliver alone, especially with what Bill had already been through that day. Bill nodded, and we walked next door together.

The horrible task of telling Chris's parents that their fourteen-year-old son had just been shot to death was left squarely on our shoulders. It was one of the most difficult things that Bill and I ever had to do.

The minister and his wife smiled at first when they saw us. But that changed quickly when they saw the looks on our faces.

"What is it, boys?" Chris's mother asked. "Where's Chris?"

"Chris is...uh, he..." Bill stammered.

"Dear God, what happened?" the minister exclaimed.

Bill looked like he was going to be sick, so I finished what he was going to say. Chris's mom screamed and nearly fell, but her husband caught her and, sobbing himself, helped her to the couch. Bill ran outside. I stood frozen, not knowing what to do or whom to help.

Chris was buried in Atlanta three days later, on Bill's birthday. After that day, we saw a permanent change in our dad. Rufus Hannah Sr. never went hunting again. Or at least if he did, he made sure nobody else knew about it.

Dad was never charged in the accidental shooting, but the verdict he charged himself with was far worse than anything the law could have handed out. Dad's punishment was to hit the bottle more than ever, drinking so heavily that the man who had raised

Jenny, Bill, and me essentially died that day with young Chris on the hunting trip.

"Pa? Pa? Are you okay?" I would often call from the doorway of the living room when I saw my father passed out on the couch, his hand clutching the neck of a bourbon bottle. I always made sure that Pa was still breathing as I pried the bottle from his fingers.

As for me, I have felt guilty about the incident all my life, even though I wasn't there and even though I technically had nothing to do with it. In my mind, if I had been there with my dad, the incident never would have happened and my life might have turned out differently. That day, the sunny side of my life started to slowly go dark. The real turning point, however, would be the next step in a pattern that had begun with a baby bottle. That same baby bottle—or the beer in it, anyway—would begin to haunt me a year later, at the ripe old age of fourteen.

CHAPTER 2

DRINKING, DROPPING
OUT, *and* I DO'S

I HAD BEEN A LONER FOR SOME TIME NOW AND MUCH preferred the company of older people to kids my own age. This led me to the local fuel-and-food stop and the loyal group who would gather round the old table.

I figured this out for the first time on a typical Georgia summer night. I was sitting on the curb outside the store, smoking a cigarette and pretending to casually observe the goings-on. If it were a movie, I could've been a slightly smaller version of James Dean, watching the world go by and checking out the action. But I was just me, a fourteen-year-old kid sitting on a curb in the shade, staying cool while waiting for someone who was old enough to drink to show up.

After about an hour of waiting and smoking half a pack, I watched as an old Chevy with a couple of guys in their seventies pulled up slowly in front of me. Another guy would later join them on foot, since he lived nearby. They went inside, chatting casually about the recent heat wave and how it affected cotton prices. I watched through the window as the men bought some bourbon, whiskey, and beer. They walked by me and then around the corner of the store, carrying their paper bags, still chatting, and not paying any attention to the kid who followed them.

Behind the convenience store, on a concrete platform lit by the store lights and some kerosene lamps, the old guys settled comfortably around the rusted table, scraping the chairs on the concrete as they sat.

One man pulled out a deck of cards and started to shuffle as the others passed the bottles of liquor around the circle. "I think we're being watched," he said without looking up.

Another man glanced over and saw me leaning against the back wall of the store, staring at them real quietlike. "Son, either come over here and join us or get back home to your mama," he said, studying his cards.

I obeyed, shuffling over to the table and sitting. The first man started to deal me into the game, but one of his buddies stopped him.

"He's too young for cards. Leave him be," he said.

So the game continued as I sat quietly, listening to the tales of the town, local gossip, weather reports, and some pretty colorful language. Finally, a half hour later, the old geezers took pity on me, this silent kid at their table. One of them handed me a bottle of bourbon under the table. I took a big swig. Dang, it felt good. I thought it was funny that they believed me to be too young for cards but not too young to drink.

The game and the drinking continued that night and beyond. The men continued to pass bottles to me, first under the table like it was some kind of secret, and then, chucking the charade, in full view. They approached it like a kindly old neighbor lady taking pity on a stray cat and setting out a dish of milk. The men never said anything about it, and hell, I didn't either; I barely said anything to begin with. Our enjoyment of the booze and one another's company somehow shrank the generation gap.

My new favorite pastime would unfortunately stay with me long past those leisurely days of rusted old patio furniture and colorful stories. I would take my drinking habit to school with me, later to work, and also into my marriages.

—

My pa was the only high school graduate in the Hannah family, by way of night school and a GED diploma. Although I was never personally motivated to finish school, I did feel a sense of responsibility to my family. When I did buckle down and go to class, I worked hard and mostly enjoyed the experience, earning a lot of As and Bs on my report cards. But for me, the biggest challenge was avoiding trouble outside the classroom rather than inside.

The first time I dropped out of high school was in the ninth grade, when I was fifteen. My family lived in North Carolina. A couple of friends and I were playing cards for money on the bus on our way to school one day. There was no bourbon at this game, but I had picked up some useful card-playing tricks just from watching the old geezers behind the convenience store. A paper bag on my lap jingling with the winnings was proof that I had learned well. I grinned when I laid down another straight. One of my buddies swore under his breath. Another made a lame attempt to end the game.

"The driver's been checking us out in the rearview mirror," he whispered. "Maybe we'd better stop for today."

"Nice try, loser," I said, shuffling the deck.

Unfortunately my buddy turned out to be right. When the bus pulled up in front of the high school and we walked to the front, the driver slammed the doors shut in our faces.

"Not so fast, boys," he snapped.

I looked out the window, and my stomach sank when I saw the

principal striding angrily toward the bus. "Damn!" I said to nobody in particular.

"I'll be sure and mention that too. That'll mean more paddling, I'm sure," the bus driver said as he opened the doors to let the principal in.

In the face of a paddling as punishment, I decided I'd much rather quit school and go home. Yeah, I made a rash decision, just like I'd done in the past—and just like I would do a lot of times in the future to screw up my life.

"Leave me the hell alone," I told the principal, and then I stormed off.

When I told my folks what happened, Pa's response was simple: "Find yourself a damn job!"

So I did, working with my father until they decided to move back to Swainsboro. Since I was now seventeen, I decided to stay in North Carolina and work, calling my folks once a week. But the tradition of family togetherness soon weighed heavily on me as Christmas approached, and I went back to Georgia, living with my grandmother at first and then with my parents again. In addition to coming home, I also went back to school at their urging.

It took a little time for me to get in hot water all over again. This time it was a windy day, and outside, in the school's designated smoking area, I found it hard to have a decent smoke with the wind blowing in my face. Some friends and I found temporary shelter around the corner. The side of the building shielded us from the wind, and we continued puffing away.

I suddenly threw my cigarette to the ground and stomped it out. "You've *got* to be kidding me!" I yelled.

My pals continued smoking, bewildered at my behavior. "What is it?" one of them asked.

The school principal—another damn little Napoleon type like the one who'd been on my case before—had found us once again. He yanked the butts out of the other kids' mouths and crushed them on the ground with my smoldering smoke.

"What in the hell do you think you're doing?" he exclaimed.

"We're only a couple of feet from the smoking area! What's the big deal?" I asked.

"The big deal is that you're making a mockery of the rules, and you need to be made an example of!" the principal snapped.

He led us back to the school. We gathered in his office to learn our punishment. I sat near the door, having decided it was time to leave again, no matter what.

"What is it going to take, boys? What do I need to do to straighten you out?" the principal said, his hands folded tightly in front of him.

The other guys stared in different directions. I could see that the thin older man with a receding hairline was getting hot under the collar. He said that he took little pleasure in this, but at the same time I knew how much the weasel wanted to humiliate us.

"Fine!" He slammed his fists onto his desk. "Fine! That's fine! I hope you boys are in the mood for some fresh air and exercise, because for the next hour you will run laps around the front of the school yard."

"Just because all the classroom windows face out there, right?" I said like a smart aleck, laughing in disbelief. Humiliation—just like I'd figured.

"That's right, Hannah. I know how much you in particular like all the attention," the principal said.

"And that's what it is? For smoking a couple of feet away from where we could smoke?" one of my buddies asked.

"That's what it is." The principal grinned and leaned back in his chair.

To nobody's surprise, least of all the principal's, I got up and started to walk out. "There goes Hannah. The coward's left the building again. I always figured you for a quitter," the principal taunted me.

I paused in the doorway, started to hoist my middle finger, and then stopped again. Getting revenge on such a loser wasn't worth it. The laps would've been embarrassing—the whole school would've been able to see me, which was probably his plan—but confirming what this old fool already thought of me would've been worse.

"He's not worth it, guys. Don't give him the satisfaction," I told my buddies before walking out.

This time I dropped out of school for good. I never really cared about earning a high school diploma, despite how much I liked going to class and learning new things. I only kept going back for as long as I did because of all that my pa did in order to finish school. I saw how important this was to my father, and I did my best to make it happen. It just wasn't meant to be. I would, however, receive my GED when I was eighteen.

Another thing made dropping out all the easier. There was one thing I would much rather be doing than sitting in class, playing cards on the bus, or chain-smoking in a designated alley: *drinking.* Starting at the age of fourteen, I began drinking hard liquor daily—mostly bourbon and moonshine—while sneaking beer from my parents. I was likely a confirmed alcoholic by the age of fifteen. If I were given the option of going to class or to work or doing much of anything else, I would almost always find a way to get drunk instead.

—⁃—

School wouldn't be the only venture that would lose the war with my love of drinking. There were, of course, the girls.

Gail Lawson was a pretty, confident thirteen-year-old girl when I met her at my cousin's place out in the country. I was eighteen at the time. My family and I would make the trip together, and as a rule, everyone would get drunk, so we'd have to stay the night. Gail frequently rode by me in a truck, giving me a friendly wave. Even from the first time this happened, I had the feeling that this wasn't just some kid making me feel welcome. Maybe it was the wink that accompanied the wave.

She seemed older than thirteen, and I figured that was a good enough reason to see where this thing was destined to go. Nevertheless, to help put my mind at ease, I sought out a second opinion—an older, wiser opinion from an older, wiser version of Gail.

Walking by the kitchen late one night, I saw my chance. My sister, Jenny, sat alone at the little table in the breakfast nook, sipping a mug of tea and flipping through her new issue of *Seventeen* magazine.

"Hey, Jenny. Mind some company?" I asked.

"Sure, why not?" She pushed the chair out opposite her with her foot, her eyes still in the magazine. I sat across from her, picking at my fingernails, my eyes roaming around the familiar old room. Suddenly the pea green appliances made my stomach churn.

"What's the matter, little brother?" Jenny asked.

"I was just wondering what you think of Gail."

"Well, what do you think of her?"

I shoved her magazine away.

"I hate when you do that, Jenny, answering a question with a question," I said.

She looked right at me this time. "Then ask me the question you really want to ask me."

"How bad is it that she's thirteen and I'm still in love with her like she's eighteen?" I asked.

Jenny thought about it for a moment. "Jerry Lee Lewis was twenty-two when he married his thirteen-year-old cousin."

"Yeah, and all hell broke loose. I'm afraid that's gonna happen for me and Gail too."

"He survived, and you will too. Love is love," Jenny said.

"So you're saying if it works for Mr. Great Balls of Fire, it's okay for me too?"

We laughed, trying to be quiet in the dark kitchen.

"Seriously, being in love with someone is never bad, Rufus," Jenny said gently.

"But Mom and Dad—"

"Yeah, Mom and Dad and the law and the people in town, they're always going to have something to say. This time it's about age, but next time it could be color, neighborhood, job, or something else."

"So that stuff doesn't really matter?" I asked.

"It matters to them, sure. But you and Gail have to decide if it matters to you."

I grinned. "What would your magazine say about it?"

"Have you even been listening to me, you knucklehead?" she exclaimed, whacking me upside the head with the magazine.

We laughed, and I got up to leave.

"By the way, what did you mean 'this time,' Sis? You think I'm going through all this nonsense again?" I asked her from the doorway.

"Life can be funny that way." Jenny chuckled again and returned to her magazine.

One day Gail and I finally had a chance to get together and chat. The age difference didn't seem nearly as important when we were together.

We continued to get along well, and soon we were on our first date at the local fair. We rode the fair rides, checked out the exhibits, listened to the music, pigged out on the beer-battered, fried, and otherwise-sugary food, and petted the farm animals on display. Other fair patrons who observed us saw that clearly the main attraction for Gail and me was each other.

As we rode on the Ferris wheel, Gail tossed her head back, savoring the evening breeze. I pulled her closer to me, kissing her from her neck upward. I half expected her to giggle like a kid when I reached her mouth, but she didn't. Instead she kissed me back, staring deeply into my eyes. Any thoughts of my parents and the townspeople vanished.

One cool autumn evening a few months later, we enjoyed the view of the farm from the open window of a barn loft. It seemed so natural to me, sitting with this girl I felt like I'd known forever, on the farm where we'd met for the first time. But as comfortable as I felt, I was totally unprepared for what Gail said next.

"Wanna get married, Rufus?" she asked casually.

I was surprised to hear my answer come flying out of my mouth with only a moment's thought. "Sure, okay."

—••—

We were wed on Valentine's Day in 1973 and remained married for seven years. We had a daughter, Stephanie, and a son named Rufus III (the III was Gail's idea). We used to go fishing a lot, and we used to take the kids with us for a barbecue after catching all those trout and bluegills.

In many ways, alcohol ended my marriage to Gail. More specifically, the way I behaved and the choices I made while under the influence of alcohol ended my marriage to Gail. I was twenty-six at the time. When the decision was between staying for another round with my buddies after work or going home to Gail, I would choose the next round. I would remember to go to the liquor store before recalling that I was supposed to be home watching my kids. Simply put, I would forget my role as a husband and father.

Gail might have been young, but she certainly wasn't stupid. She knew that this wasn't how marriage and family were supposed to work. She was an easygoing type, so her response wasn't rage or revenge (both real, adult emotions from more embittered women). She chose what naturally had to be. Our marriage, which started as an impulsive, passionate love affair, was no longer working. Just as she had asked me to marry her, Gail now asked me for a divorce.

I respectfully agreed, knowing what I had done but unable to control myself enough to stop. But leaving my kids...Well, that was maybe the hardest thing of all. I was hardly Dad of the Year material, and I knew it. That didn't make it any easier, though.

Even after we divorced, I often contacted Gail and lived with her in our old house on Race Track Street during difficult times in my life. She would even call me when I was married to my second wife and she had a boyfriend. We had a strong bond, both before and after we split.

There were, of course, other girlfriends and wives to grab my attention after Gail. Marriage number two fell more under the "had to do it" category. In 1981 I met a girl named Eva when I was twenty-six and in army boot camp for eight weeks at Fort Leonard Wood, Missouri.

Near the end of basic training, I suffered a serious injury to my arm on the obstacle course. I met Eva in the military hospital. She was also a patient there, having suffered stress fractures to her knee and leg. We kept each other company while on CQ (charge of quarters) duty, and we went out together on weekend passes.

Eva, a clean-cut Mormon woman, did not drink, smoke, or swear. However, there was one activity she would allow, and not long after we met, she was carrying our baby. If I didn't marry her, Eva said, she would be excommunicated from her church.

I was eventually given an honorable discharge for medical reasons. Always trying to do right by everyone else, I married Eva. We moved to Virginia, where her parents lived. Eva soon gave birth to a boy named Eric, my third kid in all.

One of my fondest memories was spending Sundays with Eva's dad, a heating-and-air-conditioning guy, splitting a twelve-pack of beer while we skipped out on church. We would sit on the front steps of the home where my new bride had grown up, cracking open cold one after cold one. Once again, the primary occupants in my comfort zone were people older than me—and booze.

One Sunday morning on the stoop, Eva's dad dropped a bombshell on me. "Rufus, there's something that Eva wants to tell you when she gets home from church today."

"I'm not going anywhere," I replied.

"What I meant is that I think I should tell you first."

"Does she know you're telling me?"

"No, I just feel like I've come to know you real well, and I thought you should hear it from me instead of her. My daughter says you need to leave—she's making me kick you out of the house. She's tired of the drinking, and she's even more tired of all those phone calls you keep getting from your ex-wife."

I drained the half-full can of beer I'd been nursing and stared straight ahead. The first thought that popped into my head was that, if I left, I'd never get to see my son grow up. Combined with those I had with Gail, there were a growing number of kids I would leave behind to grow up without a full-time daddy.

"Is there anything I can do to fix things and make 'em right?" I asked.

As soon as my father-in-law glanced at me and I saw the mix of guilt and sadness in his eyes, the question answered itself. I was about to be zero for two and was wondering what it would take for me to make a relationship work.

———

Soon came "marriage" number three, another tale of steamy passion, I suppose.

Out in the country once again, I met a girl named Carol. During this time I had a friend Ronnie whose dad made moonshine. (Ronnie also happened to be Gail's cousin; small world, or small town, depending on how you look at it.) Carol lived on the farm where Ronnie worked. One day on the farm when I was hanging out with Ronnie, I rode along with Carol to run an errand. On the way back, the friendly banter between us got *real* friendly.

In the front seat, Carol turned to me and said, "You know what I like, Rufus?"

"No, what?" I replied.

Grinning with a mischievous twinkle in her eyes, Carol said, "I like sex, drugs, and rock and roll!"

Not long after that, Carol and I were tearing off the sheets in her bed. This was the strongest connection that I had ever felt with a woman. Gail had a direct sort of sweetness, like a confident puppy. Eva was a cunning cat, playing with her prey. But Carol was a tiger.

Even after the fiery evening had burned itself out, the fire in my belly that Carol had lit lived on. Surely this had to mean something. I decided that perhaps the third time was the charm and Carol was the one with whom I was meant to be. The first two were warm-ups to work out the kinks before the real thing. Now I was serious about making this relationship work.

We got to know each other better and soon moved into Carol's dad's place in Wadley, Georgia. We would eventually have two sons to add to my growing disjointed brood. We never were officially married, but I preferred to call Carol my *wife* as a term of endearment. After all, marriages number one and two were cemented only with courthouse certificates, so what was the point of adding another slip of paper to the collection?

This came in handy when Carol figured out what Gail and Eva already knew: I just wasn't husband material. By now I was choosing alcohol over everything else more than ever. Poor Carol never stood a chance.

———

A self-imposing woman, a knocked-up woman, and a passionate woman were all variations of Mrs. Rufus Hannah. There were many other girlfriends and love affairs, but all were ultimately rejected for my greatest love of all: a mistress named Alcohol.

How much power over me did this mistress have? Shortly after Carol and I split, I was living with my mom—she and my dad were separated at the time—in two rooms of a farmhouse while I worked with horses on the farm. It was 1986, and I was thirty-two. I had to leave that job to serve a jail sentence for a DUI, and I'd been in jail for only a few days.

This one real confusing morning began with the warden waking me up early in my cell without telling me why, ordering me to get dressed, and then sending me out with a cop without telling me where I was being taken. The cop handcuffed me in the back of a police cruiser, and I looked out the window as the car pulled into the parking lot of a funeral home.

The back door opened, and the officer helped me out. "Up against the car," he ordered.

I obeyed, and the officer removed the cuffs. "What now?" I asked.

He simply pointed in the direction of the front door.

"What *is* it?" I snapped, growing tired of the bizarre game of cop charades.

The officer led me into the funeral home. There was a funeral in progress in the main room. Some of the mourners looked up as I entered. I glanced at them and felt my heart stop beating; I couldn't breathe. I saw my pa, Billy, Jenny, Uncle Melvin, Aunt Dorothy— my entire family. There was only one family member missing—the most important one. I swayed on my feet, and the officer had to steady me.

My legs somehow found the ability to walk into the room. The family swarmed forward to hug me. This was the first family reunion since my troubles with alcohol, women, and the law, but at the moment it seemed as if the days of moving from neighborhood to neighborhood together had never ended.

As I stared in shock at my mother's coffin, Jenny grasped my hand and squeezed tightly. The minister continued the service.

"All those who knew Lucille knew what an incredibly special lady she was. Wife, mother..."

That was when I pretty much checked out. I sat in one of the white folding chairs, staring numbly at my mother's coffin. She was really dead, and my whole life had flipped upside down. She might not have been in the parenting Hall of Fame, but that didn't matter to me. She was my mom, and she had always been there for me. Now she was gone, and I was a prisoner standing at her coffin.

It is a moment I will never forget. But had I hit rock bottom yet? Oh no, not by a long shot.

CHAPTER 3
WORKING MY WAY WEST

"FIND YOURSELF A DAMN JOB!" MY FATHER HAD TOLD ME more than once.

When I dropped out of high school for the second and final time, the words of my pa hovered over the next phase in my life.

The Hannah family work ethic quickly kicked in, and for a short time, I believed that a life of steady work was my destiny. When I was in school, I battled between two great loves: learning in class and drinking instead of learning in class. As it turned out, my job history wouldn't fare much better.

My first construction job came when I was eighteen, the initial entry on my never-ending resume in an industry that would be a continuing theme. This particular construction job paid $2.25 an hour (I ended up quitting after being refused a raise). It was 1973, and Gail and I had just gotten married. I was drawn to this industry because, on construction jobs, the men drank at lunch and then again after work, and it was considered okay. The drinking breaks became the deciding factor in answering a whole lot of want ads.

Next on my résumé came work at a sawmill in Nunez, Georgia, followed by a four-year stint at the St. Regis Paper Company, where I would become leadman. I left both of those jobs because I preferred drinking to work. Another factor in the resignation was that my girlfriend at the time (I had recently been divorced from Gail) lived too far away from my job, and I didn't want to make the trip to work. My excuses mounted in proportion to the pile of discarded wives and jobs, but I didn't notice. The world just wasn't working out the way I hoped it would, and alcohol was the best way to forget this.

The string of job entries on my résumé soon included running tractors on a farm and working at a salvage job and another construction company. I also had a job painting heavy equipment, which I left because I would rather drink. I worked as a mason's helper—same reason for resigning. I tied steel together on a bridge while working at another construction company.

Each of these jobs ended because of the pull of the bottle that had lived in my shadow since I was born. This driving force had grown steadily stronger in my teenage years; now it was finally overpowering me as a grown-up. By this point too many people knew me by name, reputation, or both. There were cops around every billboard and light post, ex-wives and their cousin's cousin's cousin around every suburban cul-de-sac, and no doubt pissed-off ex-employers lurking too. I wasn't an educated man, not book smart, but I was smart enough to recognize defeat when I saw it.

By the time I reached the end of my string of jobs, I was forced to leave Jenny's house in Tennessee, where I had been staying, because of problems with the police. I moved on to Nashville, splitting a one-room place with Bill, now also an alcoholic. We worked day-labor jobs to earn the sixty-dollar-a-week tab for our room.

The only problem was that I frequently spent our rent money on booze. After several weeks of this, Bill had had enough. He waited up for me late one night after I had been out boozing.

"This has gotta stop, Rufus. It ends tonight," Bill said.

"Fuck you. Lemme go to bed."

"Goddammit, if you don't quit spending our rent money on booze, you gotta leave!" Bill exclaimed.

I stood there for a moment, staring at Bill, and then made the only kind of decision I was prone to make: a quick one. I had my bag packed in minutes. Bill didn't seem at all surprised.

"There you go again, quittin'—you quit on school, on your wives, and your KIDS!"

Bill knew he was bound to strike a chord with me as the words came out of his mouth. But he kept yammering away as I got more and more pissed off.

"You wanna know what Jenny said after you left Mom's funeral in the police cruiser? 'No matter how many times Rufus falls down, as long as he can think of a reason to get up again, he will. He's not going to learn until he runs out of reasons. And until then—more falling.'"

"What're you tryin' to do to me anyway, Billy?" I asked.

I tried not to let on how much Bill was hurting me. Here was the last remaining family member willing to give me a second chance, and now I was watching that chance fall all to hell right in front of me. A part of me knew that everything Bill said was true and that I deserved it. But that part was quickly overruled by my stubborn, bruised ego, which was on the verge of overheating.

And then Bill delivered the final blow. "It's about time someone in the family told you what everyone else is thinking."

In the moment before my left fist connected with his jaw, Bill smiled a little, as if he thought he'd made a dent in my thick head. The last image I had of Bill was him standing there and holding his jaw as he watched me storm out and slam the door behind me.

Another impulsive decision had left me with nowhere to go, no money, and not a whole hell of a lot of prospects to speak of. But like it or not, I was committed to going out into the world.

So in 1990, I first became officially homeless.

———

I hopped a train to Louisville to try to find work just to get by. I might have been homeless, but I was lucky enough to rarely go hungry. I would go to a luncheon every day at a Lutheran church. They had the best home-cooked meals. You could eat as much as you wanted, but you always had to clean your plate. If you threw away any food, the Lutheran monk would tell you, "Don't come back for one week." That was fine with me, since my folks had taught me never to throw away food.

During my year in Louisville, I met another homeless guy named Tim, a painter by trade. We saw each other frequently at local shelters and struck up a friendship. I preferred living on the streets to the shelters most of the time. The shelters required people to be in at a fixed time, lights out on schedule, and the most frustrating rule of all for me—a chain-smoker—was that absolutely no smoking was allowed.

One evening Tim and I went to a local bar and found a couple of female friends. I clicked with Sharon. We stayed at the bar while Tim and his gal, Sandra, got cozy in a corner booth.

At first Sharon and I made small talk. Smoking a cigarette and drinking a beer, I glanced over her shoulder and saw Tim and Sandra howling with laughter, their hands clasped across the table. At least one of us would get lucky tonight, I figured. I wasn't sure yet if there was going to be a connection between Sharon and me; she hadn't shown even a little bit of that sort of affection yet. But that didn't matter to me. Sharon was interesting to talk to. So I decided to tune back in to Sharon, who was showing me photos of her kids. She had lost custody of the kids, who were now being raised by her mother, although she saw them as often as possible. Thinking about my own kids, I felt uncomfortable.

Lots of drunken laughter preceded Tim's and Sandra's return to the bar. I was glad for the distraction.

"Wanna get out of here?" Tim asked, saying what all four of us were thinking.

We returned to the fleabag motel room where Tim and I were staying. Sandra immediately flopped down on the bed and beckoned for Tim to join her. I went to the bathroom, and when I came out, the room was dark, and Tim and Sandra were already rounding third base and heading for home.

"Coming to bed yet, Rufus?" a voice called from the floor.

I looked down and, good Lord, saw Sharon lying naked under the comforter! Sandra might have been making the most noise, but I felt like I got the far-better deal. Sharon wasn't trying to prove anything— she just wanted to be with me.

The next morning we all went to a nearby coffee shop. Tim and I complained about the lack of day-labor work in Louisville. We wanted out. Sandra was also feeling restless and in need of an adventure.

"Road trip!" the excitable gal proclaimed to the table. Seems she owned this old van. "Runs good too," she added. "Come on. We'll drive it out West. It'll be fun!"

"I'm in," Tim said.

Sharon and I also agreed to go, although I wondered how Sharon would feel about leaving her kids behind. Without bringing them up, I said, "We'll just go out there and see how the work is, and if it's no good, we'll come back."

"It'll be fine," Tim said. "My brother lives in Phoenix, and he's a painter. He's been saying for a while that he can get me work out there. I just didn't know how I was going to get to Arizona."

"Lucky you met a hot chick with wheels, then, isn't it?" Sandra said.

"Yeah, it is."

———

Headed west—and with a woman—I was hopeful that this cross-country trip would go well. Although work was the main goal, I looked forward to seeing some of the country.

We left Louisville in the summer of 1991 and headed west. We worked out a system in each town we visited, first hitting the welfare office and applying for food stamps. Once the stamps came in, Sandra (our designated spokesperson and chief negotiator) would sell the stamps to local bar patrons. She was equally skilled at cadging gas vouchers, food, and other necessities from churches, shelters, and anywhere else where a little sweet-talking negotiation could go a long way.

Tim and I pulled our weight by hustling for day-labor jobs whenever possible. In Little Rock, we two natural-born workhorses met a contractor who had some painting work. He even put all of us up in a motel room for a couple of days. Unfortunately, as soon as we had settled into the free room, the rain started, and there was no painting that could be done. We kept busy by playing cards.

"You think he's gonna let us keep the room much longer?" I asked Tim.

"I don't know, maybe if it stops raining by tomorrow."

I glanced over at Sharon, who sat on the bed, talking to her mom and her kids on the phone. She might have seen the parallel that we both had kids, but shoot, I didn't see it that way at all. I never saw my kids anymore. They were being raised by their mamas and whomever their mamas were with. I didn't see anything similar about my version of being a parent and Sharon's. And I was growing concerned that this road trip wasn't worthwhile enough for her to be away from her kids.

"I was hoping to pick up some cash pretty soon," I said.

"Relax, man. My brother has it all taken care of. Plenty of work in Phoenix," Tim reassured me. So I reached for my bottle of beer.

It ended up raining for three days, so the paint job was a bust before it started. We checked out of our free room, fortunately with no hard feelings on the contractor's part, and hit the road, headed west again.

The next eventful stop occurred in Oklahoma City. Things were going pretty well by this point. The four of us got a motel room and spent the day sightseeing.

Near the end of the day, it was my turn at the wheel. Tim and Sandra slept in the back. I was glad they were sleeping, because their little lovers' quarrels had recently turned into all-out battles. It was exhausting being around them, but I was willing to do whatever it took to keep them from breaking up, since the trip itself was courtesy of Sandra's van.

Next to me in the front seat, Sharon stared out the window. She seemed to be brooding, and I had a gut feeling it had everything to do with her kids. She'd started the trip with the attitude of a kid playing hooky from school. Shoot, we all had. But as the miles added up behind us and it grew harder and harder to collect enough food stamps for a decent meal, reality set in. Phoenix and the promise of work seemed just as far away now as they had back in Louisville. I stared at the rolling plains up ahead and wondered what I'd gotten myself into—and how the hell I was going to get out of it.

At that moment it was as if the good Lord decided to put an exclamation point on my worries. A rattling sound followed by a loud bang heralded what I knew, with a sinking feeling, to be the blowing of the transmission. The van was dead on the shoulder of the road, miles outside of town, and we had no idea how we would get the money to fix it.

"Don't worry. We'll figure something out," Sandra said cheerfully.

"I don't think food stamps are going to cover this one, Sandra," Sharon retorted.

I had to laugh as Sandra glared at us.

"Come on, guys. Let's just figure something out," Tim said.

Sharon got out and started thumbing for a ride. I let her go. Tim and Sandra weren't the only couple on the road trip having problems. I leaned against the van, lit a cigarette, and suddenly wondered what Gail was up to. I hadn't thought of her in a while, and the best I could figure, the only reason she had popped into my head now was that I was teetering on the brink of losing another woman. And since it wasn't about the booze this time, I felt even more depressed. Maybe the problem wasn't alcohol. Cripes, maybe it was me.

Tim laughed. "What does she think she's doing?"

We watched Sharon sticking her thumb in the air at the empty road, and I felt jealous of her. She had a family to go home to eventually. Even Sandra seemed to have some kind of life in Louisville.

She had treated this whole trip more like a college spring break. For Tim and me, the lack of work was much more serious, perhaps life threatening, if the drought continued any longer.

"You remember back at that restaurant where we had lunch?" Sandra asked.

"You're gonna talk about your lunch now?" I said.

Sandra glared at me. "What I meant is that while we were at lunch, I overheard some people in the next booth talking about something called the Jesus House. It's like a shelter or something."

We eventually made our way to the Jesus House, a local hangout similar in many ways to a homeless shelter. Tim and Sharon lay low at separate ends of the room. While Sandra worked her moneymaking magic on one end of the place, I struck up a conversation with a fellow disabled veteran. We hit it off, and the guy offered to call around to some local junkyards to help us find a transmission. He made a few calls and finally shouted, "Bingo! Found you a transmission for seventy-five bucks, man."

I pulled out my wallet, pretending to have that amount, while hoping that Sandra would come back with a pocketbook full of cash.

"Put that away," the guy said. "I got this and the tow to the shop. You guys already have enough troubles, by the sounds of it."

I felt overwhelmed by this fellow veteran's generosity. It was great how vets stuck together. Was this a sign that my luck was turning, or was it just dumb luck? I decided to stop thinking about it and just be grateful that this man had come along when he did.

Before Tim and I headed to the repair shop, I went to hug Sharon. But she turned away and walked to the pay phone.

"She calling her kids again?" Tim asked.

"Probably," I said.

"You know, you better do it pretty soon," Tim told me. "I mean, let her go back."

"I know. Fuck off!" I snapped.

"Easy now. By the time this thing is done, we might be the only ones left standing." Tim chuckled, lightening up the mood.

I again thought about how this stranger was kind enough to help out a fellow vet in trouble. Tim was right, so I managed to calm down.

Once at the shop, we borrowed some tools from the owner and installed our new transmission.

When we returned to the Jesus House later that night, we found out that Sandra had collected eighty-five dollars in donations from the folks there. We felt like we were on a hot streak when it came to our luck and the kindness of strangers.

We left Oklahoma the next day, and things were mostly good. Sharon was even speaking to me again, showing a renewed interest in getting our relationship back on track. But rather than cheering me up, this change in Sharon actually broke my heart. It weighed heavily on me, as a dad, that she was the mother of several kids back in Louisville. I thought about this all through the journey. By the time the van pulled into Flagstaff, Arizona, I had made a decision.

We spent a couple of nights at the Salvation Army. On our last night there, I waited for Sharon in the kitchen. I watched her from around the corner as she took her photos out of her pocket and spread them out on the counter, smiling through her tears.

"Well, darlin', that makes what I have to tell you a little bit easier," I said softly, coming up behind her.

"Jesus, Rufus, you scared me." Sharon clutched at her heart as she tried to put the photos away.

I put my hand over hers, stopping her. "Too late. The secret's out. You miss your kids."

Sharon wiped away some tears and nodded.

"Listen, darlin'. Despite what it may seem like, I don't know where in the hell I'm gonna end up or what the hell I might get into along the way. We both know you'd be much better off going home to your kids. They need their mama there more than you need to be traveling in some van across the country." I hugged her.

"I'll miss you," she sobbed into my shoulder.

"I know. Me too."

I held her for another minute or so, and then it became time to get practical. How was she going to get back home? Fortunately, Sandra still had some of the donations she had collected, enough to buy Sharon a one-way ticket to Louisville.

—

The next morning we took Sharon to the bus terminal. Our foursome had become a threesome, and we continued on west. As planned, Phoenix became the eventual end of the line for the nearly two-month van trip. This was about all that went according to plan from there. Tim and Sandra's battles had transformed into all-out war. Finally, in Phoenix, the couple had milked as much mileage as possible out of their relationship. After one last fight, Sandra split and took her van back east.

Tim and I carried on with our original plans and met up with Tim's brother. But just like in Little Rock, we never got to work. Tim and his brother, much to my unpleasant surprise, were on bad terms. The argument that ensued reminded me of my last conversation with Bill. The brother called Tim a screwup and slammed the door in our faces.

With no jobs, no home, and barely any supplies or money, Tim and I were left in Phoenix very much on our own. The van had gone east, the job situation had gone south, but the two of us were still determined to make it somewhere out west.

How in the heck had I gotten to this point in my life? All that family left behind, my wives, my kids, because of…what? I'd lost everything because I couldn't quit *drinking*. Now I was on the streets and a hell of a long way from home. Could it get any worse?

Unfortunately I found out that it most certainly could.

PART 2

On the STREETS

CHAPTER 4

HOMELESS *in the* CITY

TIM AND I WERE STRANDED IN PHOENIX WITH NO JOBS and nowhere to live. As we sat in a hole-in-the-wall Mexican restaurant one day, I looked to Tim to take the lead.

"I say we go to LA," Tim mumbled through a mouthful of burrito.

"Why LA?" I asked.

"Haven't you heard, man? It's the land of endless opportunities and plentiful jobs!"

I wasn't particularly sold. Tim didn't sound any more knowledgeable about this plan than he had about any of our other plans. But the truth was, I didn't have any other ideas.

"How're we gonna get there?" I asked.

Tim pointed out the greasy restaurant window. "See those train tracks across the street? There's a train that comes through tonight headed west—straight shot to La La Land. I heard it from some guy yesterday."

"But we don't have money for train tickets," I grumbled.

"When are you going to stop thinking like a regular joe? People in our position have to be more…creative," Tim told me. "Quarter after eleven tonight, we're back in business. We get to California, there's jobs everywhere!"

By eleven that night, however, we were officially hammered. We'd found a liquor store on the way to the railroad tracks. A couple of empty bottles of red wine later, we lay sprawled on an uncomfortable bed of desert sagebrush next to the railroad tracks, staring up at the starry night sky.

"Wonder if it'll rain," I slurred.

"Dunno, maybe. Hope not." Tim lifted his wristwatch to his face, squinting to see it.

"How much time we got?"

Tim's eyes finally focused and widened. "Oh shit!" He scrambled to his feet as I followed.

"What?"

"It'll be along any minute now."

We swayed drunkenly in the darkness next to the tracks. Tim shoved me back a few feet.

"You gotta have space to get a running start," he said.

Soon we heard the rumbling of a train approaching in the distance. "Ready?" Tim asked.

I almost fell over trying to imitate a runner's crouch, but I managed to nod at Tim.

The slow-moving freight eventually reached us, lumbering across the desert. We watched the cars go by one at a time before finally spotting an open boxcar.

"Go!" Tim yelled as he ran and leaped and then landed on a ladder that hung off the car and grabbed onto a handle.

The graceful, running leap that I had envisioned performing came out more like a stumbling belly flop. Fortunately I scrambled to my feet quickly and grabbed for Tim's hand. We fell into the freight car in a heap of arms and legs, breathing heavily.

"See? What'd I tell you? The only way to travel," Tim panted as I grabbed a stitch in my side, nodding.

The next morning, when my eyes popped open, it took a few moments to remember where the hell I was. The rumbling of the massive train beneath me was a reminder. Pouring rain pounded down on the top of the freight car. Puddles of water formed in random spots around the car where the roof leaked. I looked around but didn't see Tim.

This was the first time since leaving Louisville that I was left alone to make my own decisions. I stood and looked out into the predawn darkness. It was pitch-dark, so I had to gauge how fast the train was traveling by watching the tracks whiz by below me. This made me dizzy, so I decided just to hope for the best instead.

Thinking that perhaps I had missed LA and Tim had already arrived there, I soon decided to jump. Fortunately the train was moving slowly. I crawled onto the ladder on the side of the car and was instantly drenched. Taking a breath, I leaped through the air. Luckily I didn't break any bones. After landing with a thud in the mud, I rolled for a few feet and lay there, staring up into the darkness.

I finally stood, having no clue where I was, and started to walk. I didn't know what direction I was going in, but guessed I'd eventually end up somewhere, and then I could figure it out from there. I figured this was probably the outskirts of LA and thought that once the sun came up I'd be able to see the big city's skyline.

"Hey, Rufus!" a voice in the darkness yelled.

I turned and walked blindly toward it, finally seeing Tim. He stood in front of a shack, nearly invisible in the rain and darkness. Turns out he'd jumped off the train only a couple of minutes before me. We huddled in the shack until sunrise.

When the sun finally rose, the outlines of buildings were visible in the distance. Since this was my first time out west, I didn't know how big the Los Angeles skyline was supposed to be, so again I trusted in Tim's leadership. As we started walking toward the city, we ran into another homeless man going in the opposite direction.

"Nothing in the city for you, brother?" Tim asked him.

"Not this one, man," the guy responded.

"I thought LA was the land of endless possibilities," I kidded my scowling friend.

The man laughed and looked at us like we were mental. "You're kidding, right?"

"About what?" Tim said.

"I hate to spoil your party, man, but that's not LA. It's Tucson," the man responded, laughing even harder as he clapped us both on the shoulders and walked away.

I felt the ground come up to meet me, and I hadn't even had a drink yet. "You fuckin' kidding me?" I yelled angrily at Tim.

My friend shrugged. "I guess we hopped the train going east instead of west."

"Asshole!" I was pissed over Tim's casual attitude.

"Don't cuss at me. The wine was your idea!" Tim yelled back.

"So if we weren't drunk, you woulda known east from west? That's what the problem was?"

"You were there too! You could've said something."

"You've been telling me this whole time to trust you, so why would I stop now?" I asked.

We continued arguing as we walked to town, until our hunger caused a cease-fire. We stopped for soup at a homeless shelter called Guadalupe's. Later in the day we found a Salvation Army that was sending groups of five or six guys to various churches for the night. We were placed in the same group and enjoyed a comfortable night of warm blankets, pillows, and a hearty meal made by the parish women. Shoot, we even managed to earn some money by doing odd jobs for the pastor the next day. So we decided to make the best of this temporary setback while preparing to have another go at reaching Los Angeles.

One day Tim disappeared (as he had the habit of doing) for a while, leaving me alone to dig an irrigation ditch outside the church. The young, friendly pastor joined me outside, even going so far as to pick up Tim's shovel and join me.

"How long have you and your friend been homeless?" the pastor asked.

"We're not exactly homeless," I said, "we're on our way out to Los Angeles for work, and a few things haven't gone right."

"That's understandable. Cross-country trips can be challenging," the pastor said. "How long have you and Tim been friends?"

"I don't know if I'd call us friends. We were both looking for work, so we figured maybe we could help each other out."

"That's great," he said, and we stayed occupied with our work for a few minutes.

"Where are you from?" the pastor finally asked.

"I'm from a little town in Georgia called Swainsboro," I answered.

"Do you have family that you left behind?"

I stopped working for a moment and squinted up into the sunlight, considering if I wanted to do this. I was more aware than ever that I was on the opposite end of the country from the folks I loved. I wondered if they still thought about me. The alcohol had cut through all my family bonds like acid, and I felt the sting.

"I…don't want to talk about them," I told him.

The pastor nodded. "If you ever do, you have the number here."

—

Eventually, with a little cash in our pockets, we took another try at hopping a freight train west, this time successfully. We made it as far as a train yard in Colton, California. But then, as Tim and I were playing cards with some other homeless guys, we heard a commotion outside.

"Get out! All of you! Outta my yard now!" a voice bellowed.

"Run for it!" someone yelled.

"Uh-oh," Tim said, motioning for me to follow him to the back of the car.

"Where are we going?" I whispered.

"We gotta get out of here."

Just as we made it to the door, the bulls, as the train yard security guards were called, stormed the car. They chased everyone off the train and out of the yard. Fortunately, Tim and I had enough change left to take a bus into San Bernardino, a city about an hour east of Los Angeles. We stayed at the Salvation Army there for another couple of nights.

Still following Tim's lead, I was soon watching Los Angeles pass by as we caught a bus to Santa Ana, a city about thirty-three miles farther south.

"Uh, what happened to LA?" I asked Tim, dreading the answer. Tim's continuing pipe dreams had become irritating by now.

"Changed my mind," Tim mumbled from behind a girly magazine. "I got family in San Diego. They can help us out."

I hoped that Tim was on better terms with his family in San Diego than he was with his brother in Phoenix. But I kind of doubted it. Not having any better ideas, I decided to keep my mouth shut.

So here I was, a Southern boy from Swainsboro, staring out the smudged window of a city bus at a freeway. I looked at the swarming cars, like a herd of smoke-breathing sheep being shepherded from one place to the other. I glanced up at the thick layer of dirt hanging overhead where the sky was supposed to be and wondered how the hell I got here and, more important, how the hell I'd ever get back home—or if I ever would. It was getting on toward Christmas of 1991, and for the first time I felt real homesick for my family. No matter how much they hated my guts, I just wanted to see a familiar face.

The bus let us off in Santa Ana. Out of money by now, we positioned ourselves by the interstate on-ramp in hopes of hitchhiking south. Tim's thumb wasn't bringing us any luck, so I had a better idea. I found a piece of cardboard on the side of the road and a tube of lipstick underneath it. Inspired, I scrawled a sign: Going Home for Christmas—San Diego.

Tim approved of the plan. "Good idea."

I focused all my efforts on holding the sign as high as I could. Ten minutes later a yellow Camaro driven by a Mexican man screeched to a halt in front of us. The guy, on his way to visit his grandmother in San Diego, offered to drive us there.

I arranged my rucksack into a pillow and lay down across the backseat as Tim climbed in front. Soon I started to drift off to sleep. The holiday tunes pumping from the speakers set in motion a dream I've never forgotten.

It was just before dawn on Christmas morning in Swainsboro. Jenny practically dragged me, five years old at the time, down the hall toward the living room, a finger to her lips to warn me to be quiet. In the living room, Jenny immediately scrambled to the tree, shaking and rattling presents around impatiently. I stayed in the doorway.

"Jenny, come on. We're gonna get in trouble. Let's go back to bed and wait for Mommy and Daddy to get up," I whispered.

"Don't be such a Goody Two-shoes," she retorted, sniffing a present for clues.

"I'm not...I just don't wanna ruin Christmas," I said.

Jenny looked at me. "Don't be silly, Rufus. How could you ruin Christmas?"

Suddenly I was all grown up, standing in that same doorway and staring blankly at Jenny. And just as suddenly Jenny turned into Gail and the kids, looking up at me with sadness in their eyes.

Before I could say anything, I woke up, my heart really hurting from the dream. The Camaro was pulling over along an off-ramp near downtown San Diego. Tim and I got out of the car and thanked the driver. We all exchanged holiday greetings before the yellow Camaro sped off.

As we walked down the ramp, I looked around at the city. My journey had taken a large chunk of 1991, but I'd finally made it from one end of the country to the other. I noticed that the homeless population was visible everywhere. This was disheartening to me: it meant lots of competition for food and handouts.

We walked along city streets to Embarcadero Marina Park, a small park near the harbor. I didn't bother asking Tim about his family or the alleged work waiting for us. By now I knew better. We had hardly spoken to each other since hopping the second freight train in Tucson.

Just as I had thought, a lot of homeless folks hung around the park. We watched the sailboats, yachts, and cruise ships come in while listening to the other homeless people playing guitars and—of course—drinking. I was pleasantly surprised by the relaxed, almost partylike atmosphere there. Standing there for a minute, I let the warm, salty breeze coming off the water touch my face. This seemed like a whole different planet from the East Coast.

So the two of us, the newest arrivals to the city's homeless population, settled in and bought some tequila from an entrepreneurial Mexican who sold fifths for one dollar and equally cheap cigarettes, a buck a pack. Tim and I split a bottle, drinking in silence and watching the sunset. When the bottle was empty, I stood on a bench, surveying the park for someone who would sell us more booze. No dice.

"I'll go downtown and get us some more," Tim said, gathering his things.

He turned and walked away before I could answer. It was the last I ever saw him. He had disappeared again, but this time for good.

—

Hours later, after realizing that I was alone, I looked around the park from a new perspective, as a guy truly on his own. I wondered what the devil I was supposed to do now. This didn't seem like the type of country town I was used to, where day-labor jobs could be found if you looked hard enough.

Besides, I wasn't sure I had the energy to keep looking anyway. I could no longer muster the strength to fight off what life was throwing at me. There is an expression that when a guy becomes so beaten, he could just curl up and die. In real life, it isn't that black-and-white. The warning signs had been coming for a long time. But despite my best efforts to turn things around and go back to my sunny Southern life, I was now homeless and on my own, with no plan. The road trip was over; I had arrived at my destination. And I was drunk again, this time with strangers.

Sleeping that night, I dreamed that I was three years old again, lying in a cotton field while my family picked cotton. My head was nestled on a pillowcase stuffed with cotton, rays of sunlight warming me. I opened my eyes and was blinded by the sunlight.

Then I realized that it wasn't sunlight blinding me. It was a flashlight beam. I squeezed my eyes shut.

"Hey! Get up!" an angry voice said.

I felt a nightstick poking me in the side. When I opened my eyes, it was still dark and a harbor cop stood over me. At least he had moved the flashlight. I squinted up at the cop through bloodshot eyes, then realized that I was lying on a picnic table.

"Come on. You've gotta move along!" the cop said, continuing to prod me until I finally managed to sit up.

I groaned loudly, grabbing my head in pain.

"I'm goin', I'm goin'," I mumbled, just to make the prodding stop. The cop moved on to the next homeless guy nearby to repeat his routine.

This would become a frequent scene, played over and over during most all of 1992, the year I was homeless in San Diego. No matter where I slept, the police would frequently wake me up and tell me to move on. After a year of homelessness in Louisville, then on the road in a van with three other people, and now on my own, all I wanted at this point was to be left alone. And all that I got in return was to be hassled and shuffled around like the cargo that arrived in the San Diego harbor every day.

———

As dawn rose on my second day in San Diego, I established what would soon become a daily routine. Every morning I would go downtown to a well-known church mission for coffee and breakfast. Then it was on to a homeless program nearby, where I would take a shower and wash my clothes if the line of other homeless people waiting to do the same thing wasn't too long. The center also had a television and a Veterans Administration (VA) hospital social worker on hand who would give out information and bus tokens. Finally, I got my mail and made collect phone calls to my sister from the center. The main purpose of those calls was to make arrangements for Jenny to cash my VA check and wire me the money. But I also wanted to hear a familiar voice. As hard as it was to live like this, having that lifeline to a family member was my saving grace.

For the rest of the day, I would do my best to fight off boredom by riding around on the bus, going to Balboa Park to listen to free concerts, returning to the church for an afternoon meal, and donating plasma a couple of times a week for money. Canning routes (recycling), usually a good way to make money, were not an option simply because there were too many homeless people in and around San Diego picking the trash bins dry.

I would also frequently take the trolley down to Tijuana to Ley, a superstore I liked to think of as Mexico's version of Walmart, to get some cheap tequila and cigarettes. Other than that, there wasn't a whole lot to do.

Although there were a few exceptions, most of the time being homeless is really a lonely existence. By nature a lifelong loner, I preferred to not be bothered (drinking intensified this feeling). But I occasionally found a friend I could trust.

On my first full day in San Diego, I made my way around the shelter, getting information and advice and learning the layout of the city. Two of the most helpful people were a Mexican guy named

Cruz and his girlfriend, Julia. The couple pushed a shopping cart containing all their belongings. They were both younger than I and spoke English well. Cruz had black hair pulled back into a ponytail with an elastic band. Julia's black hair, by contrast, was cut into a cropped pixie style. But there was something about their looks that could easily have made them brother and sister.

Julia had approached me while I was on the pay phone anxiously trying to pry some information about local bus schedules from a transit operator who was determined to make it as complicated as possible. I was growing anxious because I was down to my last quarter, and time was running out.

"All I'm trying to find out is…Yes, I understand that, but…I just want to know what route goes to the VA hospital in La Jolla…Hello? Hello? Dammit!" I slammed down the phone.

When I looked up, Julia was standing there, looking at me curiously. "I just wanted to introduce you to my boyfriend, Cruz," she said. "He knows his way around here pretty good, and I thought maybe we could help show you around."

I followed Julia across the crowded room. We hit it off instantly and started hanging around together.

Cruz and Julia welcomed me into their makeshift plywood home under the Seventeenth Street bridge, which was propped up against a concrete support column. We would all go out shopping, get some eggs, beans, and broth, and make nice little Mexican meals. The camp had a hole that Cruz and others in the group living under the bridge had dug, and they used it as a barbecue pit. This added scrambled eggs and other hot meals to their choices.

I didn't always stay with Cruz, Julia, and the group under the bridge, but I would visit them regularly. Other times I would take my sleeping bag and camp out in Balboa Park or somewhere else I considered safe. But to tell the truth, safety was never a guarantee.

One night I got drunk and passed out in a park on the campus of San Diego City College. I enjoyed the big grassy lawns and picnic tables there, as well as watching students as they studied. That, and the fact that I never got hassled, usually made for a relaxing day. But on that night I wasn't so lucky. When I woke up the next day, after another alcohol-induced blackout, my wallet—and worst of all, my ID—was gone. Without ID I wouldn't be able to get my VA checks or the money wires from my sister.

A counselor at the Veterans Center across from Balboa Park gave me some bus tokens and sent me up to the VA hospital in nearby La Jolla for a replacement ID. I arrived at the large hospital and got my ID sorted out in a first-floor processing office.

Also on the floor, near the drug and alcohol center, was the only smoking area—a rec room. The room would generally be active, with veterans hanging out, watching television, smoking, sharing information, and playing cards. It was in this smoke-filled room, where vets swapped tales of victory and defeat, that I met a fellow veteran named Donnie Brennan. How could I know at the time that this guy would not only become my best friend but also the bloodied, semiconscious victim of an alcohol-induced beating—at my own hands?

——

Donnie stood three or four inches taller than I and was a much more imposing man. The afternoon we met, I heard Donnie before I saw him. He was yelling at someone on a pay phone in the corner. I immediately thought of Julia and decided to see if I could help.

"Well, Jesus, how is that my fault, Ma?" Donnie yelled. "No, I won't apologize for using the Lord's name in vain, because I'm damn pissed! The only reason that bastard's trying to pin this on me is 'cuz he's got nothin' better to do than hassle me...Ma...Ma, don't hang up. Ma, I need some more mon—Dammit!"

Donnie slammed the phone down, turned, and saw this scruffy little guy smiling at him.

"And what in the hell do *you* want, asshole?" Donnie demanded.

"I...I, uh, was wondering..." I stammered.

Suddenly, offering to help the pissed-off stranger seemed like a really bad idea. Besides, I was quite sure that the only reason it had worked for Julia had something to do with her ability to flirt. I quickly improvised.

"Could I bum a smoke?" I asked.

Donnie continued to glare at me but pulled a pack of cigarettes out of his back pocket. He had two left, and he gave me one. After he lit our cigarettes, Donnie turned his back on me, walked over to a card table, and started shuffling a deck. I followed and sat across from him.

"What's your name, soldier?" Donnie asked as he dealt.

"Rufus Hannah," I told him, picking up a hand.

"What branch of the military did you serve in?"

"I'm retired army."

"How long did you serve?" Donnie asked.

"One month," I said.

"A *month*? Fuck, I spent thirteen months in Vietnam and got wounded by enemy fire. You spent a month and retired! You got to be fuckin' kidding. You're like a broken-down tank! They can't use 'em or fix 'em, so they retire 'em. You're just an old fuckin' tank, Rufus."

I laughed, still trying to figure this dude out. There was something about him that was volatile but also interesting. His charisma was intoxicating. Not like real booze, of course, but he seemed fun to be around. I relaxed a bit and that felt good. We played cards the rest of the afternoon. After that we ran into each other frequently at the VA, and I got to know his story.

Donald Gordon Brennan was born August 18, 1949. He grew up in a predominantly middle-class suburb of San Diego called La Mesa, experiencing life in Southern California in the 1950s. For me, the fifties were more a decade of transition as the Old South struggled to catch up with the new America. The Southern California tales that Donnie told in the VA lounge fascinated me. This part of the country was so different from Georgia. Where I came from, we didn't have beaches full of surfer dudes or a green flash at sunset or grunion runs at midnight (people running around on the sand, scooping up little fish that swam ashore to lay eggs). I couldn't get over that last one.

This La Mesa sounded like a good place. It sounded like a place where I might finally be able to feel at home (as much as any homeless guy could, anyway) after all these years of traveling from place to place, not really having anywhere to call home. The last home I remembered was the room I rented with my brother. I wondered how Bill was doing.

At least, in the meantime, I had made a new friend. Not that I was any more of a trusting person, but hell, Donnie was a vet, and I liked his stories. Plus, there was safety in numbers, and this was important for homeless guys.

CHAPTER 5

"MOVING" *to* LA MESA

By now it was late 1992, and I had been homeless on the streets of San Diego for about a year. Most of that time I spent by myself, minus the occasional visits with friends like Cruz and Julia and weekly phone calls to my sister, Jenny. I also spent a lot of time talking to Donnie at the La Jolla VA Hospital. We mostly discussed where it was better to be homeless: the city of San Diego, where I had been living, versus the suburb of La Mesa, Donnie's hometown. The truth was, I felt lonely in a huge city chock-full of other homeless. And La Mesa, Donnie assured me over and over, was like a large "small town."

The attention I *did* get came from the wrong people: the police. One or two homeless people together was okay and didn't attract much attention. But when they gathered in groups of three or four or more, it tended to remind folks that this is unacceptable to society. Therefore, the police would wake me when I tried to sleep next to others. They would make me walk on, like some kind of wind-up toy, causing me even more stress and exhaustion than I already felt.

When I stopped to think about it, I knew that the cops weren't doing anything outside their job description—or what was considered acceptable—based on what they thought they knew about homeless people. They were doing their best to keep the peace and protect all citizens, homeless and otherwise. But when you are one of those homeless citizens being shuffled here and there with no real place that you're *supposed* to be, it can feel like a long and endless nightmare with no way of waking up.

I often wanted to ask them, "If you don't want me here, where do you want me to be?"

So when Donnie started talking about what it was like being homeless in La Mesa, he got my attention. "Man, it's nothing like here in the city. I'm talking trees all up and down the street. It's real quiet, and there are hardly any other homeless people anywhere."

"It sounds great," I said.

We were leaning against a railing in a walkway connecting one of the VA hospital entrances with the bus stop. We'd just gotten ourselves kicked out of the lounge for smoking.

"Yeah, La Mesa's a real friendly town," Donnie said as he cracked open a can of soda.

"Hey, listen, Donnie. I've been meaning to ask you something."

I had been thinking it through for a while, ever since Donnie first started talking about this perfect all-American town called La Mesa.

"Well, go ahead and ask, then."

"Would it be all right to come to La Mesa with you and live there?" I asked.

Donnie looked at me like I was a complete idiot and went back to drinking his soda.

"Well, can I?" I persisted.

"What do you mean, *can you*? What am I, your mother?" Donnie snapped.

I briefly reconsidered my idea. The last thing I needed was another guy like Tim bossing me around.

"You can do whatever you want, Rufus. You're a grown man, so start acting like it," Donnie said. He turned his back on me and started up the walkway toward the hospital. "Of all the idiotic things to ask…"

I followed a couple of steps behind. Heck, I didn't appreciate Donnie saying I was an idiot any more than I appreciated being told the same thing by my brother, my ex-wives, or Tim. But at least I had a plan to get out of the city and back to suburban living again.

As I passed by a mirror in the lobby, I caught a glimpse of myself. Scraping by in San Diego had taken its toll on me. When I had arrived fresh from the road trip with Tim, I looked pretty much like I always had back East: trimmed hair, clean clothes. Now, after living under bridges and in parks, my hair had started to grow out of control, I had a scraggly beard, and a clean set of clothes was a long-forgotten luxury.

This La Mesa place sounded as close to back home as I could think of right now. And by now, Donnie was on board about the idea of me teaming up with him. Of course, I wasn't expecting the miracle of a clean bed, a roof over my head, and three hot meals a day. I just hoped for the slightest improvement over living in a city crowded with other homeless as well as cops who didn't want to deal with us anymore. It had become a real challenge just to survive in San Diego.

———

So Donnie Brennan and I, an unlikely pair, arrived by bus in La Mesa, where we would remain homeless for the next ten years.

Our first home was a dugout at a baseball field next to a park where Little League games were played. I quickly felt at home. It was safe enough there, with few people to hassle us, that we could leave small bags of our personal belongings under the benches in the dugout. When we were out during the day, we didn't worry if our bags would still be there when we returned at night.

Life in La Mesa exceeded my expectations. There were cook-outs with Donnie's mother, Virginia, and other family members, including Donnie's son and daughter, Joseph and Cory, and a stepson named Chris. We did odd jobs for Virginia and others— these kinds of day-labor jobs were old hat for me. We hung out at bars and pool halls and went out to eat with the money we earned. We would try to make friends with business owners and find ways of getting our laundry done and take showers at friends' houses. Staying clean was always a priority; we never wanted to sink to the level of *appearing* homeless.

After living in La Mesa for a few weeks, I caught a glimpse of myself in a mirror in a billiard hall: clean clothes and clean, trimmed hair. Things were finally changing, I figured.

At this time, during the early- to mid-1990s, true to Donnie's word, we were just about the only homeless people in La Mesa. We were tolerated by the townspeople. Many locals actually thought we were brothers, since one of us rarely appeared without the other. The local police knew us well and seldom gave us any trouble, or vice versa.

There was one exception to this, and his name was Officer Krupke. Not really, but we called him Officer Krupke after the hard-nosed cop in *West Side Story.* Krupke became our most hated enemy. He tried to make our lives miserable at every opportunity. The cop, a horrible guy, made it a point to be wherever we went, whenever we went there. He would write us an endless stream of tickets, which of course we couldn't pay. This was just to give him an excuse to toss us in jail, while meeting his ticket quota. Krupke would also frequently cuff Donnie and cart him back to Virginia, saying, "Keep your damn son!" I found this to be equally ridiculous and infuriating.

But as nasty as he was, Officer Krupke was just one cop as opposed to an entire city police force giving me trouble, as had been the case in San Diego. In La Mesa I didn't have to play a continuous game of cat and mouse with the cops.

Between family visits with Virginia and also with Donnie's kids, cookouts, regular showers, laundry, and so many locals who fondly knew our names, it was sometimes easy to forget the big differences between us and everyone else. For a while it wasn't what I would call a bad life, not by any means. The biggest advantages in La Mesa were the relationships we created within the community. Business owners chatted with us about our lives and allowed us to sleep behind their stores.

The two of us also found comfort in the friendship we built. Donnie relayed more of his life story to me. Remember, he hadn't exactly taken to me back at the VA hospital in La Jolla, but with good reason. His life growing up wasn't all Schwinn bikes, after-school garage bands, and a spoiled childhood in Southern California, which I initially believed it to be.

When he was seventeen, Donnie fell in love with an old 1956 Ford Crown Victoria and bought it from a friend for fifty bucks. Since his father, Joe, had strictly forbidden Donnie to purchase the car, the shit hit the fan in the Brennan home when he brought his new treasure home. Donnie exploded and took off out the front door.

He went straight to his uncle Dick's house (Virginia's brother) to live and work with him in the auto-glass industry at a shop he owned. One day on their way to a job, his uncle decided to have a serious chat with his thickheaded nephew.

Donnie told me the story as we finished up a game of pool in a La Mesa pool hall, beers in hand.

"So my 'Uncle Dick' [Donnie made quote marks in the air] turns to me and asks, 'Is there anything I can say to make you go back to your parents?'"

"What'd you tell him?" I asked.

"I told him no! My mind was made up, and nothing he said was going to change it," Donnie replied stubbornly.

He then relayed how, unable to avoid the inevitable for a moment longer, Uncle Dick dropped the bomb on him. "So he goes and says, 'Donnie, *I'm* your father.'"

"Oh shit. Really?" I asked, draining my beer.

"The whole family tree is suddenly all fucked-up. My mom is my aunt, my cousins are my siblings. It was a big fuckin' mess," Donnie said.

On the positive side, Uncle Dick had found the one thing he could say that would make Donnie go back home. Donnie did, and he had the biggest fight with his mother to date, wrecking the house in the process.

The real breaking point came during the argument when his mother looked him square in the eye and said, "You'll never be a man!" Donnie told me how those words burned into his brain and stayed with him, fueling the next series of events in his life.

One day Donnie borrowed Joe and Virginia's prized blue and white 1966 Chevy Impala. He parked it on a hill outside the house. Later the car was gone. Donnie had left the shifter in neutral and had failed to set the parking brake. The car had rolled down the hill, crashed through the front of a neighbor's house, and ended up in the living room. Joe was furious, and Donnie felt terrible. Later, as he sat in a doughnut shop drowning his sorrows in cup after cup of coffee, Donnie noticed an army recruiting office across the street.

"So I told the recruiter, 'Give me the biggest thing you've got to drive!'" Donnie bellowed, reenacting the scene for me as we left the pool hall.

I laughed. "Somehow it doesn't surprise me that you would say that."

Following through with his promise to show his mother that he was a man, Donnie joined the troop that would be the first in and last out of Vietnam. He enlisted two months before he was to graduate from high school, in April 1968—at the height of the Vietnam War. While Virginia was horrified by her son's sudden and dramatic decision, Joe stood at the bus station and pumped his fists in the air victoriously as Donnie left.

When a real prideful Private Brennan arrived in Vietnam, still bearing grudges for what he saw as a massive betrayal, he was more than ready to drive the biggest tank and shoot the biggest gun available. As a former athlete, he knew the importance of a good score. And the scorecard he was presented with was the body count.

Whenever the smoke cleared and the earsplitting attacks died down, Donnie and his fellow soldiers would be responsible for tagging the ears of every enemy they had killed. After each battle, sixteen to eighteen U.S. soldiers would walk back across the blood-soaked battlefield and sort through the carnage. Each American soldier would claim and tag any enemy soldiers he remembered killing. Donnie described the process to me as, "This one's mine, this one's yours."

He remembered a particular firefight in which three enemy divisions—some five thousand North Vietnamese regulars and Vietcong—charged directly at the American forces. Donnie told me,

"The battle was like a turkey shoot." On that day Donnie had twenty-six confirmed kills. He grimaced while telling me that, in comparison with the rest of his platoon, his body count was quite low.

He soon graduated from tanks to helicopters. Donnie's Chinook chopper routinely descended into notoriously dangerous regions such as Cu Chi, An Loc, and Tay Ninh. In another battle, the enemy fired a B-40 rocket carrying a 105-pound high explosive. The resulting percussion drove a piece of shrapnel deep into Donnie's left shoulder. He was in a hospital for two weeks and went back to battle at Tay Ninh. This time he was shot in the right hip by an AK-47 round. Fortunately in Nam there was always a steady supply of beer to medicate the physical and mental damage.

But the worst thing that happened to Donnie in Vietnam wouldn't be the agonizing physical wounds he received. One day the enemy had set up artillery and machine guns atop the Nui Ba Den Mountain in Tay Ninh, one of the most violent areas of Vietnam. The guns kept Donnie's platoon pinned down for three days. Donnie fought alongside his best friend in the military, a fellow named Bobby who happened to be from El Cajon, a city just east of La Mesa. Bobby, an army cook, had also trained to use the standard American assault rifle, the M16.

One afternoon, after the fighting had subsided, Bobby asked Donnie to show him the platoon's 155-millimeter howitzer, affectionately known as the Big Gun, a monster of a weapon that had to be towed from site to site. Just as Donnie walked Bobby over to inspect the weapon, enemy snipers hidden in the mountainside foliage began to fire their large-caliber rifles. Donnie screamed to his friend, "Get down! Get down!" and pushed him to the ground, attempting to shield him with his body. He was a second late. After the enemy fire stopped, Donnie nudged his friend and cried out in horror. He now had a firm grip on Bobby's headless body.

As he finished telling me this story, tears welled up in Donnie's eyes. We silently climbed down the steps into our little baseball dugout and retrieved our stuff from under the benches, settling in for the night.

"To this day," Donnie said quietly, "any kind of loud sound scares the hell out of me. After that I didn't care who died. It was little more than rabbit hunting," he told me as we watched some kids smoking weed over by third base.

—

After four or five years of being homeless in La Mesa, the day-to-day hardships began to take their toll on Donnie and me. It became harder to stay clean by tracking down free showers and laundry. To compensate, I started throwing away my dirty old clothes and buying new ones at yard sales and thrift stores. When I didn't have any money for this, I would find clothes in Dumpsters. These types of hardships made it easier to start to give up. Life was battering away at me again after a short period when it hadn't been so bad. Sure, I had continued to get drunk during these years, but there was usually enough going on to distract me from the reality of life on the streets.

The reality was that while things seemed to be improving, they were actually getting worse. Despite the cookouts, odd jobs, and best friend, I was still homeless, unemployed, and very much an alcoholic.

More than five years after Donnie and I had arrived together in La Mesa, our greatest daily challenge remained finding enough money to buy liquor. This was especially true when we compared being homeless in La Mesa back then to being homeless in the same town now.

In the mid-1990s we started seeing the first signs of the tide shifting from San Diego, as more and more homeless started showing up in this midsize suburb. We suddenly had competition as territorialism set in, and it was harder to find and make money.

But competition from other homeless men and women would soon be the least of our worries. A significant change in our lives loomed as the millennium drew to its end, and it wasn't the kind of change for which a celebration of any kind would be taking place anytime soon.

CHAPTER 6
MENDING FENCES

EARLY ONE MORNING DURING THE SUMMER OF 1999 Donnie and I were canning—collecting aluminum cans for recycling—in Dumpsters behind apartment and townhouse properties in La Mesa and other nearby San Diego suburbs. By the time we reached the back of one particular townhouse property in the area, a complex owned and managed by a man named Barry Soper, we were both in shitty moods.

I had burrowed deep into the Dumpster, running my hands through the worst kinds of garbage, feeling for any hint of metal, when I heard someone confronting Donnie, who had remained outside the bin with a shopping cart.

"Get the hell outta here!" Barry Soper yelled angrily, coming closer to the bin.

He then jumped backward as my overgrown nest of tangled gray hair popped out of the Dumpster like a gruesome jack-in-the-box. You couldn't tell where the hair on my head ended and the foul-smelling hair on my face began. Like an animal, I bared the teeth I had left at the guy, my eyes flashing. Barry might've been a bit scared, but mostly he acted pissed off. I immediately resented the little shit. How could he know what kind of crappy morning we were having?

"Fuck you, ya heartless bastard. You're ruining our canning route!" I snapped.

"I don't care about your canning route, your paper route, or any other kind of route!" the guy replied, getting even more pissed off because we refused to budge. "I want you off my property right now, or I'm calling the cops!" He waved his cell phone at us.

Donnie, still standing with the cart outside the Dumpster, proceeded to rattle off his résumé of reasons—amid a lot of *F* words—as to why the guy should leave us the hell alone. We both wore T-shirts and jeans, filthy from days and weeks of foraging through Dumpsters. Barry took another step backward, probably repelled by the smell of alcohol and a potpourri of other scents from us. Donnie whipped out his filthy VA card from an equally filthy brown wallet, informing him that we were both vets.

Indignant, the guy said, "Explain to me how any of this equates to a free pass to hang out in my Dumpster!"

"Didn't you hear what Donnie said? We're vets, you fuckhead!" I yelled.

"I don't care if you're veterinarians! Get out of here!"

After a few last parting jabs, we took our grocery cart and left, still grumbling about the self-righteous nerd who'd interrupted our canning route.

"Does he think he's just dumping us on someone else?" I asked.

"Honestly, I could give a shit about what that asshole thinks," Donnie said.

Barely half an hour later, we had circled the neighborhood and found ourselves close to where we'd started earlier that morning. Barry saw us up the street and glared at us. He looked like he was going to read us the riot act, but then he turned and walked across the street from the townhouses toward old Mr. Hawkins's house. He had been summoned.

"Buddy! Hey, buddy!"

Mr. Hawkins called everyone "buddy," including Donnie and me. Orlando Hawkins was a folksy, ninety-year-old, six-foot-tall, 220-pound Southerner who lived in a house just down the street from the townhome complex. Most days he could be found sitting in an aluminum lawn chair in his driveway, watching the world go by. He and his petite wife, Lydia, were known fondly in the neighborhood for inviting passersby to sit down and join them for conversation, and today was no exception. Mr. Hawkins, however, was also a devout Southern Baptist who had the ability to put the fear of God in you if that's what it took to make you see his way.

It seemed that Mr. Hawkins wanted to talk to Barry about the earlier confrontation with Donnie and me at his Dumpster. Still irritated about it, Barry told him his side of the story.

"So you see why those filthy bastards had no business being on my property, right?" he concluded.

If he was looking for sympathy from Mr. Hawkins, he should have known better. The old man stared him down and said, "Barry, you should be ashamed of yourself! I know those two guys. Rufus and Donnie have worked for me before. Now you're going to give them a job."

"But Mr. Hawkins—"

"But *nothing*, Barry! I'm not asking you. I'm telling you! You give these men work, and you do it now!"

The big ol' Southern Baptist suddenly turned into a preacher, telling Barry, "Jesus wouldn't like what you're doing." Barry being a Jewish guy, I'm not sure if that registered.

But once old Mr. Hawkins was done telling him off and making him feel like crap for turning his back on us, Barry gave in. He waved Donnie and me over as he told Mr. Hawkins that he would offer us jobs.

This was how we went from being bums in Barry's Dumpster to becoming Barry's employees. The terms of our employment were to show up on time and be sober. Barry figured that he'd never see us again, and his promise to Mr. Hawkins would be fulfilled. At least he'd tried, right?

But after our own little chat with Mr. Hawkins, we were careful to show up at exactly 10 a.m. the next day, ready to work. Even before we got there, I was in a bitchy mood about working for this nerdy guy. Donnie, however, didn't want to hear any of it.

"Man, it'll probably be easy work." He winked at me. "And you *know* what we can do with the money."

We arrived at Barry's office and met his daughter. Jill was a seventeen-year-old blonde, blue-eyed high school student at the time. She told us how she was working in her dad's office for the summer. I just wanted to get the formalities over with, get paid, and go back out on the streets, and I was still pissed that Donnie had roped me into this.

"Where's your dad?" Donnie asked her.

"I just called him on his cell. He'll be here any minute," Jill said.

We stood there in the cramped office amid an awkward silence.

"I'm sorry. My dad didn't mention your names," Jill finally said.

"He never bothered to ask us," I replied.

"He probably didn't expect we'd show up," Donnie said, attempting to be cordial.

She smiled expectantly.

"Uh, I'm Donnie, and this here's Rufus," Donnie added quickly.

Barry soon pulled up outside in his old 1986 European hardtop convertible. I watched him through the window as he strolled up the walk to the office, chatting away on his cell phone, something I learned that he always did. I stared at the battered Red Sox baseball cap on his head, which he always wore. I had no intention of pretending to like the little shit. I pegged him as the kind of guy who would interfere while you were minding your own business, trying to make a buck. Now, on top of all that, after he'd gone to the trouble of hiring us, he didn't even have the courtesy to show up on time.

After some awkward conversation, Barry gave Jill a twenty-dollar bill and sent her to a fast-food restaurant to buy us breakfast. While she was away, we went outside and waited. I watched Barry answer a cell phone call, and I glared at him in disgust. He glared back, looking at me like I was a serial killer.

Donnie immediately broke the tension, starting a continuous friendly chatter about living in La Mesa. He was determined to get on Barry's good side by using a combination of charm and ass kissing.

After breakfast was out of the way, Barry put us to work. Our first assignment was to rebuild some rickety old fences on the property. But before starting, we discussed salary.

"How much you gonna pay us?" Donnie demanded.

"Five-fifteen an hour," Barry replied.

That was minimum wage at the time. As soon as he said it, we both felt relieved. If we both worked eight hours, we'd make over eighty bucks, and guys like us could buy a hell of a lot with that.

He took us to a storage room and showed us where the tools were. "Would you like some gloves?" he asked.

Donnie turned and glared at him, insulted. "We're *men!*" he snarled. Then we picked up the tools and went to work. The jobs included not only repairing but staining the fences, picking up trash, and policing the spread-out property. It was hot, miserable work in the summertime, but we kept at it.

After that Barry gave us a continuous flow of projects. From time to time he visited the work site. At one point he told Donnie that he was impressed with the effort we were putting in. We dug and chopped and pulled and lifted for eight hours. At the end of that first day he handed each of us over forty dollars in cash.

"You guys certainly earned this today," he said.

"Thanks," Donnie replied as I pocketed the money and turned to walk away.

"Well, it was nice meeting you both. Thanks again for your hard work," Barry called after us.

"You say that like we ain't coming back," Donnie said.

"You mean…you are?" Barry said, looking surprised.

This also got my attention. We both turned to confront him.

"Yeah, I thought you said you had a few weeks' worth of work," I snapped.

"I did…Um…I just wasn't sure if—"

"You weren't sure if we were comin' back tomorrow," Donnie finished for him.

"Yeah. I just met you guys. What do I know?"

"You know we're homeless and we're drunks, so you figure you know it all, don't you?" I said.

"Okay, prove me wrong," Barry said before turning and walking away.

And by God, we did. Barry made a poor attempt at hiding his shock as Donnie and I arrived at the office bright and early—and coherent— the very next morning. After another fast-food breakfast, we went straight to work. The same thing happened for a bunch more days, until we had worked Monday through Friday for two consecutive weeks. We tore down the old fence and helped him haul it away. We erected a new, sturdy one, a professional-looking job. Whenever we were done, we asked if he had any other work for us. Barry later admitted that Mr. Hawkins had been right in his "employment referral." Our skill and our work ethic made him look upon us as men rather than "bums."

———

Over the next few months we completed each task that Barry assigned us with flying colors. We continued to show up on time and took real pride in our craftsmanship. In the process I felt that Barry continued to get to know us as real people. And we got to know him too.

One day Barry came to check on us as we painted a townhouse in the complex. "Barry, I've been…" Donnie started and then looked at me. I nodded. "*We've* been meaning to ask you something."

"Go ahead," he said.

"What turned you against homeless guys like us so much? I mean, you hated us from the moment you saw us."

"What makes you think that?"

"Give me a break, man. It was really obvious, you know." I snorted.

"What would you do in that situation if you were me?" he snapped.

"I'd let a guy go about his business and leave him the hell alone," I said.

"I couldn't do that, Rufus. It was my property, and I didn't want you on it. I needed to protect it for my tenants. If nothing else, there's an issue of liability to consider. Plus, someone had taken a dump in that same spot near the trash bins the night before."

Barry told us that, in the past, he'd had no interaction with homeless people, even though he'd once served on the board of St. Vincent de Paul Village, a San Diego–based organization dedicated to helping the homeless. The more we talked with him, the more we kind of liked the guy. We even came to think of him as a friend…or at least Donnie did, anyway.

———

Donnie and I worked for Barry Soper at various times throughout the rest of 1999, and we continued to get to know one another during our lunch breaks. Actually I would mostly just sit there and let him and Donnie talk. I didn't want the guy interfering with who I was today by learning who I'd been yesterday and how I got here. I simply didn't trust him, no matter how Donnie tried to talk me into feeling otherwise. I figured that anything I told him would later be used against me.

During this time, Donnie and I lived behind a Vons supermarket at Navajo and Fletcher Parkway in La Mesa, mainly at night. In the back parking lot, we had settled into a daily routine. Our morning alarm clock came in the form of the store's large cargo door rolling up and an employee rolling out cart after cart of one-day-old food: breads, cakes, and more. Shortly afterward a BMW or some other fancy car would pull up, and the owner would fill the car with goodies from the carts. I guess making the car payments must've been a challenge. We would have our turn once the carts of remaining food were transferred to the Dumpster. Then, if we weren't working for Barry that day, we would set off on our mission to raise enough cash to buy the booze that would ward off withdrawal.

One night behind the Vons opportunity knocked for us to earn some cash and alcohol on a regular basis. This new opportunity wasn't like the usual day-labor jobs with which I was so familiar. This was not Swainsboro, where men would work side by side in the sun, using their hands to build and fix things to better the lives of others. This was Southern California, and this kind of work was custom made for it. In sunny Southern California, there was one super popular type of temporary day job in an industry more famous than any other: making movies.

Film work—the California dream. But this particular type of film work would not come with all the glamour and dazzle of Hollywood. No red carpet here. Only a dark nightmare that, for the longest time, would have no apparent end.

PART 3

RUFUS *the* STUNT BUM

CHAPTER 7

ENTER *the* BUMFIGHTS

Bumfights filmmaker Ryan McPherson lived less than a couple of hundred yards away from Donnie's mother in La Mesa. But the only similarity between Ryan's experience living in the town and Donnie's—and later mine—was geographic.

Ryan's and Donnie's respective childhoods in La Mesa might have been just as privileged. At least, that is, until they split off at the moment that, in his words, Donnie's family tree became "scrambled eggs" and the Vietnam War seemed like a better option than trying to unscramble it. Around the corner and down the street about thirty years later, there was no Vietnam to escape to. Also, you'd have to figure, none of Ryan's friends had had their heads blown off as he held their motionless bodies.

Ryan and his pals, including an older buddy, Zachary Bubeck, and later friends such as Las Vegas residents Danny Tanner and Michael Slyman, would eventually plan a series of makeshift documentary films called *Bumfights*.

Ryan's and Donnie's paths first crossed at a park near a middle school in La Mesa where skateboarders frequently hung out, along with us local homeless. Ryan, with arms covered in tattoos and dark hair that was usually overgrown and a bit messy, enjoyed filming skateboarders and anything else that caught his attention around town. One night he had his video camera pressed to his face, taking in the scene. Most of the homeless folks paid him little notice; some even went to great lengths to avoid the nosy lens of the camera. One fellow, however, seemed to delight in the spotlight.

As he would later tell the story to me, Donnie was drunk as usual and also persistent, begging Ryan to film him. Ryan finally agreed, just to make him go away more than anything. Donnie performed for the camera, drunkenly stumbling around the park and tripping over any kind of available obstacle. Ideas started to percolate in Ryan's head.

"My name is Donnie Brennan, and I'm a United States military veteran," Donnie slurred enthusiastically into the camera.

"Are you from around here, Donnie?" Ryan asked from behind the camera.

"Born and raised here in La Mesa. Went to Grossmont High School and studied hot rods there," Donnie continued, getting excited by the attention.

"Oh yeah? I go to Grossmont," Ryan said.

"Is that a fact? Well, let me tell you about that place..." Donnie rambled on for a while about the school, comparing notes with Ryan.

By the end of their encounter Ryan had expanded his filming interests from skateboarders to the homeless. Later that night, as he uploaded his video footage, he looked at the older Grossmont graduate. Why was this guy still hanging around the town where he grew up? These questions sparked McPherson's interest enough that when his economics teacher assigned the class a video project with a topic of the students' choosing, Ryan immediately thought of Donnie and decided to "document" homelessness in La Mesa for his assignment.

That's how it apparently started, anyway; that's the story Donnie told me before later introducing me to Ryan.

From the moment Donnie met Ryan, Donnie had been talking his ear off about me. "I'm serious, Ryan. If you think the shit I do on camera is cool, you're gonna love my best friend, Rufus!" Donnie would repeatedly tell him.

The two got together around town, sometimes filming skateboarders, and more often homeless people and other "freaks," as Ryan would call them. Realizing that Donnie was much more agreeable when he was drunk, which made him a better film subject, Ryan soon started buying booze for his new friend.

One day the two were drinking beers on a loading dock behind a Vons supermarket where Ryan had a part-time job.

"So where did you meet this guy Rufus?" Ryan asked Donnie.

"I met him a few years ago at the VA hospital in La Jolla. He's been talking about wanting to meet you and audition for your videos."

"Well, bring him on over. We can make him a film star too—a professional stuntman," Ryan joked.

"I think he'd be great for that. He mentioned something about running into trees to entertain kids once. I swear he likes this kind of thing," Donnie said enthusiastically, trying to impress Ryan.

"Then let's get him," Ryan said as the two clinked beer bottles, toasting their future success.

This is how I entered the next phase of my life, scooped off the streets of La Mesa with the promise of being kept continually fed, drunk, and later famous. Initially I didn't give a rat's ass about the last part.

Donnie told me about Ryan and his friends and their upcoming class project about what it was like being homeless. I wondered how a kid could do that. To be honest, I thought that being a film star was a ridiculous notion for two guys who slept on a concrete platform behind a grocery store, trying to ward off alcohol withdrawal and starvation the best they could. (Somehow I didn't see these as conflicting needs.) But if this kid was offering a package deal that came with the basic necessities, sure, then. Why the hell not? "I guess it's time to be a movie star," I told Donnie.

In reality, Ryan's plan was to make us untrained, inebriated stuntmen—not that Donnie or I knew the difference. All we knew was that these kids wanted to buy us booze and give us a little extra money, usually five bucks per stunt, all for doing some stupid shit on camera. That sounded easy enough.

Ultimately, because of the filmmaking stunts, Donnie and I stopped showing up at Barry Soper's townhouse complex to look for work. At the time Barry had no idea when—or even if—he would ever see us again. In the meantime we were being well taken care of by Ryan and his pals.

———

My new life began one night in the back of a Vons parking lot in La Mesa. When Donnie and I lived there in the late 1990s, it was pretty quiet at night. I preferred it that way. The nighttime silence always made me feel like we were alone, cut off from the rest of the irritating world. Yeah, I knew everyone saw me as a dirty, desperate drunk who was sprawled on the hard concrete platform and downing forties of liquor. But lying on my back, staring up at the quiet night sky, I could forget all the bad stuff and find comfort in pretending I was back in

Swainsboro, watching the sunset from the top of the barn with my first wife, Gail.

I would think about stuff like this especially on cold nights, when there was little to rely on for comfort. This one transformer on a concrete platform gave off tremendous heat and therefore came in handy on such nights. Once, Donnie passed out and fell asleep while leaning up against the transformer to stay warm, and he burned his arms.

Despite such frequent incidents of semiconsciousness or being out cold, we spent a lot of time wide-awake behind the store. We were often too restless and sometimes afraid for our safety to sleep for long periods of time. We became trusted resources for the local police as night watchmen of sorts. We'd long since become familiar faces to many, if not all, of the local cops. Homeless guys like us reminded me of night owls. They always see what's going on and get to know the people responsible for it. That made me even more pissed off when cops like Officer Krupke hassled us. Without guys like Donnie and me, they'd have to install security cameras in every alley and parking lot in the city.

On one such night we kept watch as usual. "You sure he's coming?" I asked my pal.

It had been nearly a day since my last drink, and *cranky* couldn't come close to describing how I felt. Withdrawal had started to set in, and every part of my body ached. The tremors and sweating would begin shortly. I dreaded what would happen if I didn't get my medicine soon.

"Yeah. He's coming," Donnie said. "Relax, man. I've known Ryan for a while, and he's never gone back on a promise yet."

"He'd better not," I said.

I passed out after that. Later, the sound of a car pulling up got my attention. I propped myself up painfully on one elbow and squinted down from the dock. Once my sight cleared, I saw Donnie standing at the window of an SUV and talking to the driver.

"Rufus, get over here and meet Ryan!" he yelled, waving up at me.

I winced with the pain of a million muscle aches as I hauled myself onto my feet, but I still managed to scramble down. Limping over to the black SUV, I was greeted by a young kid with dark black hair swept over half his face and a cocky-ass grin that I immediately could relate to. This guy was me at seventeen.

"Hi, I'm Ryan. You must be Rufus, the professional stunt bum." Ryan shook my hand through the window.

Laughter floated out from the rest of the car, and I saw another guy in the passenger seat and two girls in the backseat, still giggling and gawking at me like they were at the zoo. This made me nervous at first, but then Donnie laughed along with them and slapped me on the back, which made me feel better.

"I ain't no professional anything. I'm just a bum like Donnie," I muttered, my eyes looking down at an oil stain on the pavement.

"Either way, I've heard a lot about you. Donnie says you might be interested in being in my movie about homeless people that I'm doing for school," Ryan continued, still smiling.

I shrugged and shifted uncomfortably back and forth on my feet.

"Come on, Rufus. This is the kind of thing we've been waiting for," Donnie encouraged me.

"I don't know what the fuck you all are talking about," I said, feeling the tremors kick in. "All I know is I need a drink real soon."

"How about this? If you do some stuff for the film, I'll get you a six-pack of beer," Ryan said.

"Okay." Damn, had the need for alcohol gotten so bad that I had to do crazy, maybe dangerous shit just to get it?

We gratefully drained the six-pack that Ryan bought for us, not even caring about how a guy that young could've bought it. Then we did some stuff for their film.

Ryan told me to climb into a shopping cart. I did, and Ryan's friend gave me a push, sending me hurtling down a short flight of hard, unforgiving concrete steps leading from the back of the store to the ground. My body slammed into the pavement. Before I could even finish yelling out in pain, the metal cart fell on my chest, knocking the wind out of me. Crumpled on the pavement at the bottom of the stairs, gasping for air, I looked down and saw that my right pinkie finger was bleeding. I wiped it on my already filthy jeans and then grabbed for the beer that Ryan held out for me, then drained half of it in one gulp. Serious pain needed serious medicine.

Even in my drunken state, I realized that this could have been much worse. I could've easily broken my neck or crushed my skull on those damn steps. Bottom line was that I needed the beer Ryan offered—badly. I was grateful for the beer, but what the kid made me do to get it was really messed up. Still, since Donnie was pals with him, and I trusted my best friend, I was willing to give this Ryan kid the benefit of the doubt.

—

When Ryan showed up at Vons again a few nights later with more scenes for his class project, La Mesa's newest stunt actor—me—was plenty game. But I did have one question for Ryan.

"Don't you want Donnie in any of these?" I asked Ryan as he set up the next stunt.

Donnie was across the parking lot, hamming it up for Ryan's usual posse of female groupies.

"Yeah, of course. But I already have a lot of footage of him from before I met you. Besides, you're having fun, right?" Ryan slapped me on the back.

"Yeah, okay," I said hesitantly, quickly adding, "When's Danny coming back with the forties?"

Before he could answer, Ryan's friend and fellow filmmaker Danny Tanner, in town from Las Vegas, rounded the corner with shopping bags full of booze. Relieved, I rushed over to get fueled up for the night's activities.

The main event was a headfirst run into a towering wall of plastic storage bins. Properly plied with beer and laughing on and off at the ridiculousness of the situation, I crouched at the end of a loading ramp leading to the bins and did my best imitation of a sprinter's crouch. Ryan, Danny, and the girls, who had gone from being Ryan's posse to my cheering section (which I actually enjoyed), laughed and cheered me on.

"On your mark…Get set…GO!" Ryan yelled, imitating a race official.

I barreled up the ramp and headfirst into the unyielding wall of milk crates. Bouncing backward, I landed on my back, temporarily blinded by flashes of white lights that started in the back of my skull and worked their way around the rest of my head. Once again crumpled on the concrete behind a Vons in pain, I suddenly became aware of laughter—loud, raucous laughter. I looked up through the haze of pulsating white lights and vaguely saw Danny aiming the camera lens right at me, with Ryan and the girls throwing back their heads with laughter. It finally occurred to someone to ask if I was okay.

"How you doin', buddy?" Donnie slurred drunkenly with a big grin on his face as he helped me up.

The world still spun around me, but after another forty, I wasn't feeling any pain.

"Ready for the next one?" Ryan asked.

"Hell yeah. Bring it on," I mumbled almost incoherently.

———

I survived that night and lived to see another day—and another scene in the film. The stunts only got worse after those nights behind Vons. But for now, Ryan had what he needed. I wondered if there was even a high school class project about homelessness in the first place. All I knew was that Ryan was soon back again to film some more stunts. And we were doing stuff like belly flops into two feet of water in someone's Jacuzzi or getting shot in the ass with water balloons— even boxing with the filmmakers. Although none of us threw hard punches, Donnie and I wound up on our asses a few times.

So now we were totally dependent upon Ryan for booze and money for booze. Obviously Ryan had his own addiction to contend with. The more dangerous the stunts got, the more he wanted to push the envelope. I hated having to rely on this damn kid to keep from getting sick, given the crazier and crazier stunts he was making us do—especially me, mainly because I was more agreeable than Donnie.

But I had hit rock bottom when it came to my mental state and my desperate need for alcohol to keep my body functioning. Booze had become so important to my body that basically all I could think about from the time I woke up to the time I went to bed was how important it was to find that next drink. I knew shit like that would sound like a weak excuse to the average person, but unless they had been through it, there's no way they could know what it was like going cold turkey from something that was as vital to my bloodstream as the blood itself. I imagined it was like minor surgery without anesthesia. That wasn't something I particularly wanted to go through anytime soon. These messed-up, dangerous stunts and this cocky kid were the only things between my feeling good and my feeling like death.

Donnie and I were huddled against the transformer for warmth one chilly night when the familiar SUV pulled around the corner. This time, though, Ryan was alone.

"I wonder where the rest of the film crew is," Donnie said.

"As long as he has beer, I don't really care," I said.

Ryan walked quickly toward us with a big smile on his face.

"What's up, Ryan?" Donnie asked.

"I'll tell you what's up: Bum Fight Krew. That's what!" Ryan said.

"The fuck's that supposed to mean?" I muttered.

I tried hard to speed along the conversation to prevent my withdrawal pains from getting any worse than they already were. Our cash flow was down to nothing, so Ryan's frequent visits with gifts of food, booze, and even monetary donations were our only lifelines at this point. We would've loved to do more work for Barry, but even if he'd had any odd jobs for us at the time, his number one, steadfast, not-to-be-broken rule was that we had to be sober and coherent.

"*Bumfights* is the idea I had for all this extra film footage, and the Bum Fight Krew is all of us—you guys too—who are making the movies. You guys are real stunt actors now," Ryan told us.

Donnie laughed. "Great, when do we get paid?"

"What do you need?" Ryan whipped out his wallet.

"Man, I was just joking," Donnie said.

"No, seriously. We're all gonna be rich." Ryan handed over some small bills.

"How the fuck do you know all this?" I asked. I was charged up now by the sudden appearance of the booze money. But I was still wary. Sudden strokes of fortune like this just didn't happen to me. In fact the last time I could remember was back in Oklahoma at the Jesus House with the free transmission. Maybe Ryan was being nice like the veteran I met that day. Except that guy didn't make me run headfirst into storage containers to get the free transmission.

"I've been showing some of the preliminary footage of the stuff you've done so far at some bars. People are freaking out. They love you guys!" Ryan exclaimed.

"And we're gonna be rich!" Donnie said.

"Let's go get some beers and celebrate!" I added.

We scrambled off the loading dock, still hooting and hollering, and went around to the front of the store to go beverage shopping. Our miniparty would go on for a few more hours before Ryan finally took off for his nice, warm bed in his parents' home. Donnie and I returned to the dock and huddled up against the transformer for heat.

Ryan would turn out to be partly correct. This preliminary footage was to be the foundation for the multimillion-dollar *Bumfights* video series. With my early stunts, plus some additional footage including actual bum fights that Ryan had been filming around the San Diego area, the teenager and his friends had stumbled upon a gold mine. They discovered that watching drunken homeless people beat the crap out of one another and go flying down concrete steps curled up in a shopping cart had massive entertainment value for the segment of the American public who were into that kind of thing (the "people who slow down to look at a traffic accident" demographic, as much as I could figure).

I soon figured out that the homeless were easy targets for sick freaks to take their stress out on and use for a cheap laugh without fear of punishment. To most people, homelessness meant laziness, addiction, mental illness, or something else that was the homeless person's own damn fault. But it sure as hell didn't mean doing the kinds of crazy things that Donnie and I were now doing on an almost daily basis.

—

"What the hell's that guy doing?" I asked, pointing at the screen on a laptop that Ryan had brought over.

A naked, drunk man on a roof yelled incoherently at the camera.

I was watching Ryan and Danny review and edit footage for the school project, or the movies they were going to get rich making, whichever the hell it was. Ryan seemed to be trying to prove to me that *Bumfights* was a real movie. I didn't much care about that. I was just happy to be sitting and drinking a forty.

"Well, Rufus, what that young man appears to be doing," Danny quipped, "is standing naked on a convenience-store roof."

"That's a dumb thing to do, man," I grumbled.

"You see why your scenes are so much better? At least you're doing stuff," Ryan said.

I grinned. "I hope you pay me more than that guy once we all get rich."

"You got it, buddy."

Danny switched videos, and we were now watching a homeless guy smoking a crack pipe, going on and on about how aliens dropped him here. Ryan and Danny roared with laughter, making fun of the guy. I joined in halfheartedly, more because of the beer than because of the fool in the video. In truth I felt bad for the poor guy, but I felt like if I told Ryan this, it would piss him off. I didn't want to risk losing the money and the booze that came with the stunts.

"That's Blaine," Danny said as the guy proceeded to bang his head repeatedly against a telephone pole to demonstrate the resilience of the chip in his forehead that the aliens had apparently implanted before they left on the mother ship.

"You know him?" Ryan asked me.

"We don't have a club where we all know each other or nothin'," I said.

"That's not what I meant, and you know it—"

"Hey, there's a familiar face," Danny interrupted, pointing to the screen.

Donnie stood on a roof and rained rocks down on another bum.

"Now him, I know. That's Homer," I said.

"A friend?" Ryan asked.

"Nah. Just some dude we're always runnin' into around town. Donnie doesn't like him much because he rats us out to Officer Krupke to save his own ass."

"Figures. He seems really into it," Danny said.

I laughed uncomfortably again, hoping they'd let me keep hanging around, watching videos and drinking beers. Donnie was visiting with his mother, and I didn't want to go back and sleep behind the Vons all by myself.

"Are you guys going to be around on Thursday?" Ryan suddenly asked.

"Why? What do you want us to do?" I asked.

I was still nursing a sore neck and back from the last series of running into stationary objects, alternately falling and being pushed down steps, and other stunt scenes for the movie.

"Nothing. I just thought I'd come by and celebrate Thanksgiving with you," Ryan said.

"Uh…Okay. Sure. I'll tell Donnie," I replied, caught off guard.

It was late on Thanksgiving Day when Ryan finally showed up, toting Tupperware containers filled with leftovers from his family's holiday meal earlier that day. The three of us settled onto the concrete dock and dug in. This was the first big meal for Donnie and me in a long time, and we devoured it like starving animals. Ryan also supplied some bottles of wine for the occasion.

Once the Tupperware was empty and the wine bottles lay drained on the ground, we leaned back against the building and relaxed.

"Hey, you know what? You guys never told me how you became homeless," Ryan finally said.

"A homeless person sneezed on us, and we caught it," Donnie said sarcastically.

Ryan rolled his eyes. "You know what I mean."

So we two bums of La Mesa opened up. Donnie told Ryan all about his scrambled-eggs family tree, Vietnam, his war buddy's head getting blown off, and of course the thing that tied it all together and left him out on the street in front of his mother's house looking in: the booze.

Long into the night I told my story of jobs and marriages drying up because I always chose alcohol whenever I reached a significant fork in the road. I didn't feel much like telling Ryan about any of this. So my voice would trail off, and I would stare ahead into space with glazed eyes, and then Donnie would jump in and finish my thoughts. Hearing Donnie tell my story—one bad choice after another, with a trail of loved ones left in my wake who didn't do anything to deserve what I did to them—made it far worse. Images of Jenny, Bill, Gail, the kids, and my parents flashed through my mind. Finally I stopped talking entirely and drank the bottle of vodka that had materialized from Ryan's SUV.

"What's on your mind, Rufus?" Ryan asked me.

"Gail."

"Your first wife? What about the others?"

"She was my first love," I slurred, totally drunk again.

"And Stephanie and Rufus too," Donnie said, referring to my kids with Gail.

"How old would they be now?" Ryan asked.

"I suppose they'd be all grown—in their twenties or something?" I screwed up my face from the effort of trying to do the math.

"I have an idea," Ryan said. He scrambled off the platform to his car and a minute later returned with his trusty video camera.

"Oh, come on, man. You said we didn't have to do anything tonight!" I protested.

"No, it's not what you think." Ryan whipped out his cell phone.

"What're you up to?" Donnie asked, now equally suspicious.

"Do you know her phone number?" Ryan asked me.

"Nah. I haven't talked to her in years."

"Well, what about Jenny's?"

"Yeah. I talk to her all the time." I gave Ryan the number.

Ryan dialed, picked up the camera, aimed it at me, and handed me the phone. Half-awake and fully drunk, I took the phone without argument.

"Hello…Oh yeah. Hi, Jenny…Sorry to wake you," I slurred.

At first Jenny and I talked about the usual stuff, like how I was doing and things happening with her family. But Ryan quickly got impatient.

"Ask her about Gail!" he snapped.

I obeyed.

"Are you sure you really want to know, Rufus?" Jenny asked.

"Yeah, sure. Why not?"

So Jenny told me all about Gail: her new husband, her new life, and everything Stephanie and Rufus III were up to and what they had accomplished in their young lives. Funny, they were still babies in my mind.

"That's great about the kids. If you talk to them or to Gail, you be sure and tell 'em I said hi and I love 'em," I said, attempting to sound coherent as Ryan caught the whole scene on film.

"Rufus?" Jenny's voice sounded strained.

"What?"

"Gail doesn't really talk to the kids about you. She hasn't for a while—as soon as it was clear you weren't coming back, actually."

"Well, don't they wonder about me or ask questions?" I asked her. I tried to keep from shaking, but I did a lousy job of it.

"Not really," she said, adding the final blow. "In fact, as soon as they became teenagers, they started telling people that their daddy was dead if people asked. It was easier than trying to explain...Well, you know."

"My kids think I'm dead?" I asked, my head spinning.

Ryan grinned from behind the camera, hardly able to control his glee at the unfolding situation. I couldn't understand why the prick was grinning like a fool when my heart was breaking. This was the most pain I'd felt in a long time, and I didn't know if I could take it. I don't remember much of the conversation after that or hanging up and handing the phone back to Ryan. All I could think about was my kids, especially my firstborn, my baby girl...

Stephanie was born on a Wednesday. Gail and I were living with her parents at the time. One Monday night we borrowed her folks' car and stayed at a motel for some alone time. The next morning Gail went into labor, and I panicked. I didn't know what the hell was going on. My first thought was to get her to her sister Brenda's house. Brenda had two kids already, so I figured she knew more about this than I did. I loaded Gail into the car and just about crashed it getting there.

"Don't worry, Rufus. Since it's her first kid, there's plenty of time," Brenda said.

I was relieved to hear that, especially since the obstetrician we'd been seeing was eighty miles away in Augusta, Georgia.

When we arrived at the delivery ward of the hospital, I looked around in awe at all the women in labor. Gail's mother soon showed up. It was now 8 p.m. on Tuesday night, and Gail had not yet delivered. The doctor stopped her labor and sent her for some tests to see if she was ready to have the baby.

On Wednesday night, the doctor finally brought me the good news: "Congratulations. You have a healthy little girl."

My breath caught in my throat. I was a father. I had a little girl who was going to rely on me for almost everything for years to come. I would spend a thousand dollars that Christmas, my little girl's first, spoiling her. And when she stood and took her first steps, I would burst out laughing at the look on her face.

—•—

Now, a couple of decades later, my precious baby girl considered me, her daddy, as good as dead. That was actually how I felt now—like the ghost of the man I'd once been, who I'd drowned in a bottle.

"Turn the camera off, man. Come on," Donnie urged Ryan as I stumbled back to the wall with tears in my eyes, feeling sick.

I knew I couldn't deal with this by just sitting here. "No, keep the damn thing on. Keep rolling. Let's go do something!" I suddenly yelled.

"Really?" Ryan asked.

"Yeah, I gotta forget about that whole conversation. Give me somethin' to do, Ryan," I urged, quickly adding, "but first give me something else to drink."

Ryan looked like he'd stumbled upon pay dirt. "Come on then," he said, and the three of us piled into Ryan's car.

Soon I was perched on a windowsill looking down at a concrete pathway several feet below. I knew it was stupid. I knew I was going to get hurt, that I could get badly injured. But in my mind those things didn't seem too real. I just wanted to jump and get this over with.

Something about this was suddenly familiar. I remembered when I was six years old, playing on the family porch. At that point of my life, I'd never heard of Superman. Comic books and certainly big Hollywood movies weren't all the rage in Swainsboro. I didn't need outside inspiration like that anyway. When some kids get into trouble, they emulate a land of make-believe. When I got in trouble, it was because I felt like it. And right then this crazy six-year-old felt like jumping.

But in a way I was playing Superman that day, whether I knew it or not. It was easily a three-foot drop to the ground from the porch. The jump itself might have meant only a couple of bruises or maybe a twisted ankle. But I landed on a broken glass gallon jug. I looked down and saw my foot sliced open, skin and tissue dangling off my ankle. The grass and the porch soaked up most of my blood, yet I didn't immediately understand the impact of what had happened. I vaguely knew I should be feeling pain, but no pain registered in my head. I just sat there, staring at my mangled foot, watching the blood pour out and wondering what the hell to do next.

My mom had heard the crash and came running out of the house.

"Mommy, I—" I started to explain needlessly.

She took one look at me, sprawled on the ground and gushing blood from a partially torn-off foot, and lost it. Once she started screaming hysterically, I got scared and started to cry too. My mom quickly called a taxi, bundled up my mangled foot in a bedsheet, and off I went to get the damage repaired. My foot was never the same again.

Now, perched on a windowsill and drunk beyond all belief while Ryan held up his camera, I looked down at that foot and remembered the day I had jumped off the porch.

"You sure about this, Rufus?" Donnie called.

"Might as well make it a matched set," I said.

So I jumped. But I was no more graceful now than I had been at age six and didn't even come close to landing on my feet. I crashed to the ground, landing on my side and then rolling onto my back.

"Arrrghhh!" I screamed in pain.

It felt like somebody had snapped my spine in half like a dead branch. Shooting pains traveled down my legs to my feet. But at least it muted the pain I felt after talking to Jenny.

"You okay, Rufus?" Ryan asked.

I rolled over and tried to focus on the kid. All kinds of colors blurred my vision. It looked like Ryan was reaching a hand down to help me to my feet. I shook my head.

"You got some vodka for me?" I said.

CHAPTER 8
FILM STARS

THE PRELIMINARY VIDEO FOOTAGE HAD RECEIVED RAVE REVIEWS from guys in bars and kids in the school yard. This onetime school project was evolving into a bizarre moneymaking business venture. Not long after that, I started seeing *Bumfights* posters with my picture on them in Ryan's apartment and also posted all over the city on electrical boxes and telephone poles, especially at intersections. At the time I had no idea just how big this had already become.

Encouraged, Ryan kicked up the official shooting a notch. As the potential cash that the videos would bring in increased, so did the risks associated with the stunts—and the danger to Donnie and me.

One day Ryan took me to a towering concrete ramp under one of the largest freeway overpasses in La Mesa, overlooking several busy commuter train tracks. I stared up at the concrete mountain looming over me, taking special notice of the thick, round pillars at the bottom. The stunt that would occur here—by far one of the most dangerous—would be one that will forever haunt me, filling me with shame and disgust whenever I think of it.

I was plastered (as usual) from the liquor supplied by Ryan and friends. They made sure that I drank every last drop, because the drunker I was, the easier it would be to talk me into doing stupid, crazy things like this.

On that day they persuaded me to lie flat on my back on a skateboard. Just like with the shopping cart, they gave me, their film star, a push. Off I went, rolling at breakneck speed directly toward one of the humongous concrete columns and the train tracks only a few feet beyond. By a small miracle I drunkenly rolled off the skateboard before it smashed into one of the support columns.

In the midst of my body roll, I landed on my left arm and cried out in pain. As it was, I couldn't usually straighten the damn thing out. Now, at the bottom of the concrete ravine, my arm throbbed like hell.

This is a crappy way to treat an army veteran, I remember thinking. The railroad tracks and freeway overpass dissolved as I started to pass out with a memory from the past seared in my brain…

———

One Tuesday morning in 1981 the Swainsboro deputy sheriff unlocked the door leading to the holding area in the local jail—the drunk tank. He stood over a sleeping man's unshaven face, which was bruised from a scuffle with other local barflies the night before.

"Hannah! On your feet! You're sprung!" he shouted.

I jerked my head up painfully from the bench I'd been sleeping on and attempted to focus enough to stand up and walk. When I tried to answer the deputy, I found that my mouth had turned to cotton.

I figured Gail must have sent me here. Gail and I had recently divorced, and I believed that I'd eventually get back to living with her. But that was just a fantasy. For one, Gail had a boyfriend. Two, by then I drank heavily and was usually drunk around her. She would call the cops and have her unemployed ex-husband put in jail for the night.

My friend Danny, who just happened to be in the army, would frequently come to my rescue, and indeed he was the one rescuing me that day. Minutes later I squinted at the blinding sunlight as I walked out the front door of the jail with Danny and nearly stumbled down the steps. Danny grabbed my elbow, and we eventually made it to his car. My friend handed me a can of juice, and I swallowed it.

"Thanks, man," I said. "How's Gail?"

"She's pissed off, Rufus. More than usual," Danny answered bluntly as we drove off.

"I'm sorry."

"I know. Gail knows. Your family knows. We all know you're sorry," Danny said.

We reached a stoplight, and I said, "I don't know what to do. There's nothing here for me anymore except memories that just keep messin' with my head. I can't take it anymore."

I was talking about the trouble I seemed to face everywhere I turned: the drinking, police hassles, and general frustration with my life in Georgia. It was like being attacked by an automatic tennis-ball machine from every angle and all the time. At this point I was doing my best to swat away the incoming balls. Eventually it would be easier to curl up and stop fighting. For the moment, however, I still had some fight left in me, and Danny recognized that.

"I think I might have a solution," he said. "Uncle Sam needs you!"

On August 24, 1981, I enlisted in army boot camp. I remembered the date because it was my daughter Stephanie's first day of school. She wanted her dad to take her to school, and it broke my heart that I couldn't do this as I rode off toward basic training at Fort Leonard Wood in Missouri.

My intentions for joining the army were good. I hoped to receive training to become an electrician, a job that entailed less manual labor than the work I usually did and could lead to good money. But once again, although my intentions were good, it was the rest of me that had trouble keeping up with the demands.

This particular storm came during my fourth week of basic training. It had been pouring all night long. One morning my platoon marched out to a morass. The obstacle-course grounds were saturated with several inches of standing, murky water and even ponds beneath each barrier.

"Are you kidding me?" I muttered under my breath to a recruit at my side.

Most men joined the military as young boys of eighteen or nineteen. I had enlisted as an old guy of nearly twenty-seven.

"What's the matter, ol' man? Not up for a challenge?" The kid snickered.

I gritted my teeth. I'd been enduring these kinds of insults since the day I had arrived. And my platoon wouldn't let up. They made fun of my out-of-shape body the first time I undressed. They gave me shit about the thrift-store outfit I showed up in and just about everything else.

My fellow soldiers and I began the obstacle course. I wriggled on my stomach through several inches of mud and filthy water, feeling more like a pig than a man. The steel monkey bars felt like they were covered in grease, and I nearly slipped off several times. But I was determined to prove that my age didn't matter, and my raw anger to get back at my platoon mates drove me forward.

I finally arrived, muddy and sopping wet, at the last obstacle: a ladder stretching fifty feet above me. That slippery, mud-covered ladder was the only thing between me and graduation with the rest of the company.

Fueled by determination to finish what I'd started, I made it up the ladder, swung my leg nimbly over the other side, and broke a personal speed record for the climb down. Recognizing the moment, I stopped a couple of feet aboveground. In celebration of my victory, I performed a double fist pump, showing off for all those cocky little shits who were gazing up at me in shock.

"Yeah! Yeah!" I bellowed at the top of my lungs.

I got so busy celebrating that I lost my footing on the slippery ladder. I fell, with no chance of catching myself on the way down. The young guys in the platoon were no longer laughing. They rushed to help me.

My left elbow had caught on my hip as I fell, and the full weight of my body crashed down on my left shoulder and arm. It only burned a little at the time, so I thought it was okay. But later, as I bent over to tie my boots, searing, white-hot pain shot up my arm.

The army doctors performed surgery on my arm, but one of them forgot to send me to physical therapy afterward. I had a painful recovery, and the arm never did heal correctly. I was declared incapacitated and honorably discharged from the army in May 1982.

When I regained consciousness at the bottom of the concrete ravine next to the train tracks, I looked down at a throbbing left arm, which still wouldn't properly straighten. I knew I'd soon run out of miracles if I didn't watch myself. If I had not rolled off the skateboard when I did, I could've crashed into one of those concrete pillars and died.

By this time someone in a nearby office building had seen what was going on and called the cops. When Ryan and his friends heard sirens in the distance, they took off and left me behind. Damn kids

just left me! Another homeless guy—I later learned his name was
Mark Oldfield—had seen what had happened, and he helped me out
of there before the cops showed up.

"Why did you do this?" Barry Soper asked me sometime later, after
Donnie and I finally told him about the *Bumfights* movies.

"Because I was drunk, I got a cheering section, and suddenly I felt
important," I said.

Ryan and his friends regularly called me their movie star. They
doted on me and exhibited me like some exotic new creature in a
weird version of show-and-tell. But for me, the strongest lure of all
was to do whatever it took to ward off the horrors of alcohol withdrawal—not to mention how I was suddenly getting the same amount
of money for just a few hours of stunt work as it would normally take
a whole day or more to earn by canning. The difference: running
headfirst into a Dumpster versus climbing into it.

—

Soon the *Bumfights* filming settled into a routine. Ryan would pull
up behind the Vons at night, track down Donnie and me, and ask
us if we wanted to make some money. If we were the perfect combination of drunk enough to agree but sober enough to walk, Ryan
would cart us off to a stunt location with his friend Danny usually
behind the camera.

Many times bystanders who saw the stunts unfolding, or noticed
us hurting ourselves or each other, would get worried and call 911. By
the time the police arrived, Ryan and the other filmmakers and their
cheerleaders had scattered like cowardly mice into the night.

One time, however, Ryan stayed behind after we had duked it
out on camera to fight his own battle with a concerned bystander.

Ryan was shooting us in front of a local flower shop. The filming day had actually begun next door at a doughnut shop, where Ryan and his friend Travis filmed us trying to apply for a job and eventually smashing doughnuts in each other's faces.

Ryan had also intended to have me read off some statistics about American unemployment into the camera. They never quite got to that scene, because Ryan had a better idea. He pulled me aside.

"Hey, you know, I think Donnie got more screen time than you did in the doughnut shop this morning," Ryan whispered.

"Yeah? So? We still get the same amount of beer, right?" I snapped.

"Sure, sure. But that's not what I mean. You're supposed to be my stunt bum, the star of the movie, right? You're not going to let him steal your spotlight away, are you?"

"So what if I do?"

I was tired and pissed off. The only reason we'd stuck around after the doughnut-shop shooting was the hope that Ryan would buy us enough booze to make it through the night.

"I'm just saying, we might not need both of you after a while, so I'm gonna have to pick who's doing more stuff," Ryan said in a lousy attempt at being casual.

"What is it you need me to do, Ryan?" I asked angrily.

"Why don't you go on over and pretend to pick a fight with Donnie?"

"Pretend? Well, if it's pretend, shouldn't we be telling him too?"

"Nah. The scene will be better this way—with the element of surprise," Ryan said.

After a couple more minutes of convincing, and with the camera rolling, I barreled up to Donnie and slugged him in the stomach. Up until then we'd been doing crazy stunts and comedy routines. Now, for the first time, *Bumfights* had turned into real fighting.

"What the hell was that for?" Donnie demanded.

"You keep stealin' my scenes, you lousy bastard!" I yelled.

I was pretty sure I'd gotten the line right, just the way Ryan told me to do it. I wanted to get this over with.

"Oh yeah? Who got you those scenes, you son of a bitch?" Donnie yelled back.

I was relieved that my friend seemed to be playing along.

With that, we started brawling while Ryan and Travis laughed and cheered us on. Fortunately, we didn't do any serious damage to each other.

"Get 'em, Rufus! You show him who's boss!" Ryan yelled from off camera.

"Don't let him get away with this, Donnie!" Travis urged.

We continued to lightly kick, punch, scratch, claw, and hit each other and roll around on the ground in front of the flower shop until a woman came storming out.

"Cut it out, all of you, or I'll call the police!" shop owner Kathleen Miller yelled.

We paused and looked up at her blankly, blood dripping off my nose.

"Hey, keep going, guys; nobody said cut," Ryan ordered us.

"Yeah, don't mind her. She's just a bitch," Travis said, and the two punks laughed cruelly.

"I said stop it! It's inhumane and immoral what you're making them do!" the irate woman persisted.

"Nobody's making them do anything! Now get back inside before we burn your flower shop down, you fucking fat bitch!" Ryan yelled, losing control.

Donnie and I remained frozen midfight, momentarily at a loss over what to do next.

"What are you guys doing? Get back to work!" Travis motioned for us to continue fighting.

"They start fighting again, and I call the cops," Kathleen said, not backing down.

"Then say good-bye to your shop, bitch. Why don't you just stay out of my business anyway?" Ryan threatened.

Kathleen spun around, went back into her shop, and picked up the phone.

"What's the matter with you two? Didn't I tell you to keep fighting?" Ryan yelled at Donnie and me.

"Hey, man," Travis said to Ryan. He motioned toward the store at Kathleen, who was on the phone with the police.

"Yeah, you're right. On second thought, let's get the hell out of here," Ryan said.

Donnie and I looked at each other, nodded, and walked away quickly. Neither of us had ever seen Ryan this pissed off, and we didn't want to push him any further.

By the time the cops arrived, Ryan and Travis were long gone. Kathleen filed a police report about the teenagers who had made the bums fight in front of her flower shop.

Later that day the La Mesa police tracked Ryan down at his parents' house (someone at a business next to the flower shop had recognized him) and had a little chat with him. He denied everything Kathleen had said. He described how he and his friend were filming a "Grossmont High School video on unemployment" for their economics class.

"And who are these guys that you were filming?" the cop said.

"Rufus and Donnie—you know, those homeless guys that hang out behind the Vons?" Ryan said.

"Yeah, we're familiar with those guys. They're both alcoholics, and I'd personally recommend that you stop associating with them," the officer said sternly.

"I'll keep that in mind. Should I go down and apologize to Ms. Miller or something?" Ryan mustered his best show of sincerity.

"Stay away from there," the officer warned. "And stay away from those bums too. Find a different school project!"

"Yes, sir," Ryan said.

Of course he was lying.

That same winter of 2000, Ryan and Danny took me into the nearby mountains, supposedly to go skiing. Being from the hot and sunny South, I was curious about this whole skiing thing. And since the beer had already been loaded into the SUV, I went along with it. Of course, once we arrived, Ryan magically thought of a much better idea—especially since there were no ski slopes in these particular mountains, barely forty-five minutes east of La Mesa. People from San Diego and the surrounding suburbs, where it never snowed, always flocked to the mountains whenever there was any snow on the ground. Turned out that the footage from skateboarding down the concrete hill had come out so well, Ryan thought it would be cool to do the same thing on a slope with a snowboard.

The first couple of times down the steep, snow-packed hill were uneventful. At the end of each run there was a cold beer waiting for me. That was my only incentive for lifting up my tired and bruised body and hiking back up the hill again.

The third time down wasn't the charm. I felt every part of my body hit the cold, hard snowbank as I slid down the icy slope, out of control. At the bottom my face smacked directly into a big rock covered in snow.

The pain stung. But I only realized how badly I was hurt when I looked down and saw blood dripping from my face. At this point I looked directly into the camera that Danny pointed at me, blood dripping down my beaten face, barely able to hold myself up on my knees, and whimpered, "Please stop," similar to the way a beaten child would beg for mercy.

Other people had been sledding and playing in the snow nearby. Now a woman approached, staying out of range of the camera.

"Is he all right?" she asked with concern.

I looked anxiously back and forth between Ryan and the woman, afraid he would go off on her like he had the flower-shop owner. I held my breath as the blood continued to darken the snow underneath me. Fortunately Ryan chose a different approach for this intruder.

"Yeah, he's fine. He likes this kind of thing. He's having fun," he replied cheerfully.

I let out a breath, the hope for rescue draining from me along with my blood. As much as I needed the liquid rewards from the stunts, lately I had been secretly hoping that a concerned bystander would somehow rescue me.

I didn't know how much more my body could take. But even knowing that I felt this way didn't give me the courage to stand up to Ryan—or Donnie—and tell him that none of this was worth it.

—◆—

I was frequently the main star of the film scenes. This was usually because I was more plastered and willing to do the most dangerous stunts. But Donnie played his part too. Unfortunately for him, two of the times he stood in for me left him branded and scarred for life.

The first time was early in 2001. Ryan approached me behind the Taco Bell where we sometimes hung out, asking if I was up for doing some stuff as usual. But it was late at night, and I was so drunk I couldn't stand up. So they moved on to Donnie, who was also lying inebriated on the ground. It took a couple of tries, but Ryan and his friend Zach Bubeck were finally able to get him to respond.

"I need you to do a stunt," Ryan said, shaking Donnie's shoulder.

"Nah, go away," Donnie mumbled without opening his eyes.

"You friggin' chicken. I need you to get a tattoo, just like in Vietnam," Ryan persisted.

"Nah, let me sleep," Donnie muttered again, this time opening his eyes.

Bubeck waved two one-hundred-dollar bills in Donnie's face, more money than they had ever given us. "Come on, you coward," he said as Donnie finally hoisted himself up.

"Gimme some vodka first. You know, liquid courage," Donnie told Ryan.

This was more of a dare than a stunt, making Donnie the ideal candidate. All it took to finally get him to agree was to tell him he wasn't man enough to go through with it. That was the magic phrase that got him to Vietnam and into every form of trouble since then. Donnie got drunk enough to have no memory of what would happen that night, but he was not so plastered that he wouldn't be able to play his part.

Ryan, Bubeck, and Donnie got in Ryan's car and headed to El Cajon Boulevard in San Diego to a tattoo parlor called Inkers. After the two punks shelled out two hundred dollars in cash, a tattoo artist proceeded to inject lead ink (the most toxic and hard-to-remove kind) into Donnie's forehead. They gave him a tattoo in huge black letters that Donnie will forever be branded with: BUMFIGHT with a detailed image of a beer bottle next to it.

Ryan said it was to commemorate their film project and the infamous Bum Fight Krew, for which he was already creating merchandising. As far as Ryan was concerned, Donnie and I could be walking billboards for the franchise, considering we spent most of our days wandering around La Mesa.

All Donnie remembered the next morning were the bandages on his head and being plied with beer at the tattoo parlor. The branding remains on the decorated Vietnam veteran's forehead to this day because it would take twenty-eight separate, painful, and expensive laser surgery procedures and skin grafts over six months to remove it. (Donnie decided it wasn't worth the trouble and always wears a trucker's hat instead.). He would also eventually get A BUM LIFE inked onto his stomach, Ryan's homage to the late rapper Tupac Shakur's Thug Life.

Later, I would infamously get the letters B-U-M-F-I-G-H-T tattooed across my knuckles—the knuckles that would permanently disable Donnie in a Taco Bell parking lot. This is the other stunt that haunts me forever. My attack on that day would produce one of the most infamous images of the *Bumfights* video series, one that would make it onto the cover of the DVD, posters, and eventually into worldwide coverage.

Ryan and his friends decided to see how far they could literally take the name of the video: *Bumfights*. What would make for better filmmaking than to have the film stars engage in a live, on-camera fistfight? This would be the fight of all fights.

Of course I was stone drunk that night. And of course Ryan and his friend were egging us on from off camera, as they had done at the flower shop. They pleaded with and challenged me.

"Know what, Ryan? I don't think Rufus is *man* enough to throw the first punch!" Zachary Bubeck said. It had only been a few minutes ago when the idea of beating the shit out of Donnie, which the kids suggested, had sounded like the world's most stupid idea.

"Yeah, he's afraid Donnie will whip his ass!" Ryan replied. "But I don't think Donnie's playing along either. He's not a team player. He's going to ruin the project for all of us, and you're not going to make any money, Rufus."

"What the hell do I care about the money?" I snapped.

Bubeck laughed. "No money, you can't buy any beer."

The monster inside my gut that needed alcohol so bad roared at me. It warned me that these punks were right: I *needed* the beer that they were taunting me with. I needed it really *bad*. I'd already downed a whole lot more like it so far that day, but I knew that those would eventually wear off, and then my body would hurt like hell from withdrawal if I didn't have another one soon.

They continued to goad me, trying to get me to throw the first punch so they could capture it on camera.

"Donnie isn't one of us like you are, Rufus," Ryan continued, trying to get me to hurt Donnie some more. "He's messing up the film. He's not cool like us."

But I didn't care about none of that. All I saw in my mind were the painful sweats, tremors, and muscle aches I would have to endure within hours if I didn't get that goddamned beer.

So I tuned out and laid into Donnie, landing punch after drunken punch—hard. I beat the crap out of the best friend I had ever known.

I punched, kicked, and slapped the one guy in the world who had never let me down.

Earlier in my drunken state I thought that this was like the flower shop, where Donnie would be in on it, and the two of us would play along for the camera and not do any serious harm to each other.

But then Donnie looked directly into the camera lens, clearly in agonizing pain, similar to the way I did in the snow, like a desperate child begging to be saved.

"Please…I need 911!" were the only words that came out in a sad whimper. At the time I still had Donnie in a choke hold. Freeze-frame: instant marketing poster for Ryan and heartbreak for me when I realized just what the hell I had done.

The filmmakers did finally call 911 for Donnie, and the sounds of sirens are heard in the background of the film because they shot the EMT vehicle arriving. Ryan called "cut"—but just temporarily. Only weeks later Donnie was out of the hospital and in a wheelchair with his broken leg encased in a cast, being pushed down the street by Ryan and pissing the whole way, laughing loudly and drinking a beer.

—

The following month, in March 2001, the Bum Fight Krew went on the road for the first time. Ryan and his friends Monty and Tommy took Donnie and me north to Beverly Hills. This wouldn't be the most eventful road trip we would take, but it was…well, interesting.

Ryan, Donnie, and I were hanging out at a pool hall, drinking and playing, Ryan's treat, when Ryan told us about the trip. I cracked up as soon as Ryan told me. I thought this was the strangest "stranger in a strange land" tale I had ever heard: my pal and me being dropped in the middle of the fanciest city in California.

"Beverly Hills?" Donnie said, guffawing loudly.

"Seriously, guys, there's this chick Tommy knows who thinks she's some kind of porn star. She invited us up and told us to bring you guys," Ryan said.

"That's what she said?" I asked.

"She said bring the bums," Ryan admitted, smirking.

Donnie nodded. "Well, that's as good an invitation as any."

So north the caravan went to see this woman, whom we'll call Desiree Larue. Donnie and I were outside her building, arguing about just what the hell we were doing there, with Ryan filming as usual. I suddenly realized that we were being watched and looked up. A young girl wearing only her underwear and batting her eyelashes at us was leaning out of a window over us. She looked like a hooker.

"So these must be the famous stunt bums of La Mesa?" Desiree Larue yelled down.

"Live and in person!" Donnie replied, toasting her with his beer.

Less than thirty minutes later Ryan was crouched at the foot of Desiree's bed, filming her as she seductively stripped off her bra, performing for the camera like a stripper in training. Ryan positioned Donnie and me on the bed like crash-test dummies, lying on our backs and looking up at Desiree. This was boring for me, so I just stared at the ceiling, not sure what the hell I was supposed to do. Monty and Tommy sat in the corner of the room, drinking beers and laughing at the bizarre situation. Donnie let out a giggle next to me.

"What?" I mumbled.

"This is really messed up, man. How the hell did we end up in Beverly Hills staring up at these cow tits?" Donnie spit out between giggles.

This set me off, and we both collapsed in laughter.

"Come on, guys. Isn't she turning you on?" Ryan said from behind the camera.

I laughed. "Not really."

"You stupid asshole, what do you know anyway?" Desiree snapped, covering up her breasts and retreating to the bathroom to get her clothes.

"Thanks a lot, Rufus," Ryan said angrily, putting his camera down.

"What the hell am I supposed to do? Start sucking on them like a baby?" I snapped back, still wiping my eyes from laughter as Donnie grabbed some beers.

"You're supposed to do whatever Ryan tells you to, you stupid bum," Desiree said as she emerged with a robe on.

"Ah, shut up. We're just having some fun with you, honey. Ryan's our friend," Donnie said, laughing.

Desiree laughed back. "That's not what he's telling me—"

"Come on, guys. Let's just chill and have some drinks," Ryan said, interrupting her.

That's what we did, and the more we drank, the less we saw of the porn queen.

———

The evening in Beverly Hills had been generally harmless. But by the time we returned to La Mesa, the police were starting to pick up the trail of blood and broken bones from the other filmed stunts. Unfazed, Ryan and his friends came up with a new plan. He knew that if he continued to push me down staircases, out windowsills, down ravines and icy slopes, and provoke Donnie and me to beat the hell out of each other, it wouldn't be long before he'd probably end up in jail. The La Mesa Police had talked to Ryan a number of times, but they had just warned him. Now, he knew it was getting out of hand—especially since a nurse at the hospital had grown suspicious of Donnie's injuries after I'd beaten him up.

Toward the end of 2001, it was time for another road trip. We would travel to a city where everything goes, what happens there stays there, and the kinds of things that happened in *Bumfights* would barely cause anyone to bat an eyelash. With Donnie and me, his two film stars, in tow, Ryan and the other filmmakers set off for Las Vegas.

CHAPTER 9

SIN CITY

THE FIRST VEGAS ROAD TRIP WOULD BE THE SHORTEST AND least eventful of all the trips we made to the City of Lights. In December 2001, Ryan was on winter break from college. He and his friends remained on the La Mesa Police's radar because of the flower-shop incident and Donnie's subsequent injuries. That might have been the main reason for the trip to Vegas. But Zach Bubeck also pointed out that Vegas had a lot more action, more homeless people to videotape, and generally more types of crazy situations in which to put Donnie and me.

Before we left for Vegas, Barry Soper found us hanging out at one of our regular haunts. He now had some idea of the crazy stuff we'd been into since we had worked for him.

"This is my cell phone number," he said, handing me a small piece of paper. "If you're ever in trouble and need to get away from this punk McPherson and his cronies, you call me. I mean it. I'll put you up somewhere in La Mesa."

As I put the paper in my wallet, Donnie said, "Ah, don't worry, Barry. We'll be fine."

We didn't tell him that we were about to leave town.

When we got to Vegas, Bubeck checked us into a cheap motel on the edge of town, and the real fun began. Following orders as usual, Donnie and I got drunk. We rode the roller coaster at the Strip's famous New York New York Hotel, yelling our heads off and making fools of ourselves for Ryan's camera. I figured it was a miracle that we avoided puking on the kids around us.

We were equally fortunate during an indoor-skydiving escapade at another Vegas Strip attraction. The kids got us really drunk and zipped us up in these big suits. We carried on like crazy while these big fans held us up in the air, annoying the hell out of other people until they finally threw us out.

Getting drunk was required before all the stunts. My body needed some booze on a daily basis. But the amount of beer, vodka, and other liquor we drank before the stunts were to numb my mind against the humiliation and sometimes pain of what was to come. The humiliation was the worst, for damn sure. We were being made fools of in public, and it always made me feel sick to my stomach. One night Donnie and I had to put on wrestling costumes and run up and down the Strip as the camera rolled. I swear to God I just wanted to sink into the pavement and die as people pointed and sneered in disgust.

Another one of the infamous *Bumfights* scenes filmed in Vegas had the two of us dressed up in neon zoot suits. We hung out of the sunroof of Ryan's SUV and yelled obnoxiously at people on the Strip, stuff like, "Hey, yuppies!" "BFK" (for Bum Fight Krew), and obscenities, mostly sexual.

I was so drunk I don't remember much of the night. But what I do recall is burned vividly into my brain.

Traffic moved real slow along the Strip. This gave me a chance to take in the sights and sounds of this strange city. Through my drunken, blurred vision it appeared as a spinning kaleidoscope of hallucinations. Neon lights swirled together with an endless, pulsating sea of faces set to a soundtrack of noise, loud goddamned noise: car engines revving, horns honking, music pounding, people yelling and laughing, most nearly as drunk as I. It was like I'd been sucked into a strange tunnel where someone had cranked up the volume on the craziest soundtrack ever.

One night while cruising down the Strip and soaking in the noise, I suddenly remembered how quiet it had been in the woods the day I let my dog Rex run free for the last time. Every last leaf had settled down. It was so peaceful there, with the sun slicing rays through the trees overhead. Shoot, it was like heaven.

"Hey, Rufus, tell that chick over there to suck your dick," Ryan yelled from inside the SUV.

I raised my head, which felt like a twenty-pound bowling ball. I tried to focus my eyes on the rapidly spinning sights and felt like I was going to throw up.

"Tell her, Rufus, before the light turns!" Bubeck yelled.

Laughter floated up through the sunroof. Donnie had crawled back in and was downing a forty.

"Suck my dick!" I yelled obligingly. The girl looked up and gave me the finger.

Suddenly I found the entire situation ridiculous—hysterically ridiculous. Even the sound of my voice was funny. It sounded miles away from my brain, and that was funny too. But even more, it was disturbing.

"You wanna get your dick sucked? Suck my dick! Suck my dick!" I started yelling over and over and laughing.

The people inside of the SUV roared with laughter, and for just a second I enjoyed the attention. Then the light turned green, and the SUV jerked forward, causing me to lose my balance.

That was pretty much the most fun thing that happened on our first trip to Vegas—assuming that was your kind of fun. But the next series of trips, and the events leading up to them, would be a whole different story entirely.

———

It was now well over two years into the shooting of the *Bumfights* videos, and the La Mesa Police remained on the hunt for Ryan McPherson and his fellow filmmakers. A lot of this had to do with another homeless guy, Mark Oldfield, and his quest to become the most famous bum of all, even surpassing Rufus the Stunt Bum, as I was called. Mark was the guy who had helped me out after the dangerous skateboard stunt. He was a drug addict, not an alcoholic, and because of that, he didn't look homeless—not like Donnie and me, anyway.

By this time the first of what would be a series of *Bumfights* videos had already been released for sale—although Donnie and I didn't know this—and Mark heard opportunity knocking. He saw how Ryan was busy making Donnie and me stars, and he wanted a piece of that fame. But Mark wasn't interested in lying on a skateboard and barreling toward a concrete pillar or any of the other life-threatening stunts that I had become famous for. No, sir. No, this fool wanted to be famous for the *fight* part of *Bumfights*.

Mark began looking for Ryan so he could force his way in front of the camera. Even though he'd helped me that day, he actually admired the work that Ryan was doing. After harassing Donnie and me, he was finally able to track down Ryan. The plan was for Ryan to take

Mark to a gas station to film a scene with us. But when we went to pick him up, he wasn't there. "What the hell?" Ryan said.

We sat in the SUV next to a local park for over an hour and waited for Mark. "We gonna keep waiting or what?" Donnie asked.

"Nah, he had his chance. Let's get outta here," Ryan said and drove off.

This didn't sit well with Mark when he finally did show up. Still intent on being the new star of *Bumfights*, and now pissed that we had left him stranded, he decided to track down Donnie and me later that night to do the originally scheduled fight scene. He thought that if he auditioned for us, word would get back to Ryan about how great he would be for the videos, and Ryan would make him a star.

Mark found us sleeping in one of our old haunts: the parking lot of a Mobil station.

"Where's McPherson?" Mark bellowed, waking us from a sound sleep.

We poked our heads around the corner of the building to see what the hell was going on. Oldfield pounced like a cougar and began pummeling us. If we hadn't been half-conscious and recovering from another night of binge drinking, the fight might have been two against one. But Oldfield, more than likely on something, had the clear advantage, and he beat us mercilessly.

He knocked Donnie out first with a hard blow to the head. Oldfield then went to work on me, grabbing my skull like a soccer ball and slamming it repeatedly into the asphalt. After a quick, blinding flash of light and an explosion of pain in my head that felt like my skull was splitting down the middle, I passed out cold.

Both of us ended up in the hospital because of the attack. Donnie went to Sharp Grossmont Hospital in La Mesa, while I was rushed to Donald N. Sharp Memorial Community Hospital in San Diego, where I needed twenty-one staples to close my head wound.

I was never really the same after that. The world always seemed to be covered in a confusing, dizzying haze, which was made worse by any movement. Add my usual daily dose of booze, and I could barely remain on my feet without the world tipping over. This left me feeling frustrated and angry, often resulting in temper tantrums that exploded before I could stop them.

Mark eventually got his wish: Ryan put him in the videos. To do this Mark had nearly killed me and left Donnie in a wheelchair, but at least he had caught Ryan's attention. Mark would then take copies of his videos around to local bars in La Mesa and ask the staff to show them, telling everyone how he was a movie star now.

Meanwhile Donnie and I remained hospitalized for three days, and the authorities were getting suspicious. When I didn't seem to have a clear explanation as to how I had gotten beaten up, a nurse figured that something was wrong. She alerted a social worker, who quickly called the cops. After a lieutenant interrogated us, the police finally had the answers—and the names—they were looking for. This confirmed some of the earlier reports.

Ryan McPherson was soon a wanted man, and once he learned this his plans to go to Vegas for an indefinite time were quickly hatched. The district attorney was considering a formal investigation, and if that happened, Ryan's days in La Mesa were numbered.

Oldfield had been arrested and was awaiting trial. So Donnie and I, now back on the streets, didn't need much convincing to leave town with Ryan. We weren't exactly best friends with the La Mesa Police either. Around that time we two best-known bums were getting hassled by the cops in La Mesa nearly every day, and it wasn't just

Officer Krupke now. Things had sure changed since the days when he was the only problem we had to deal with. We tried to hide wherever we could and have a beer, but inevitably the cops would track us down, pour out the beer, and write us tickets. I thought that was a crazy thing to do, since homeless guys didn't have any money to pay fines. I had learned enough about the police to know about ticket quotas, but I still thought the whole thing was stupid, and more than that it was just plain irritating. I felt like the cops were messing with us because they could.

So when Ryan, along with his friends Zachary Bubeck, Danny Tanner, and Michael Slyman, offered to take Donnie and me back to Vegas, get us an apartment, and pay our expenses—while we did some additional filming for the videos, of course—we agreed.

—

There would actually be two separate trips to Las Vegas in 2002. During the first trip, as Ryan arrived in the scorching desert city with Donnie and me in tow, I overheard him calling up one of his buddies and bragging, "Well, I got 'em—I smuggled them in!" I felt like we were nothing more than circus animals that were being carted from city to city to do more tricks for the camera. I also knew Ryan was making money from the videos because of the cash he suddenly had to spend in Vegas and things like the "company vehicle" he took us around in: another brand-new SUV.

Ryan and Zach shelled out the necessary dough to keep us, their star performers, on the outskirts of the city in a number of cheap motels. This was a much more convenient arrangement than it had been in La Mesa because they knew exactly where we were at all times.

We filmed more scenes in Vegas than in La Mesa, because Ryan and his friends didn't have to go looking for us. We were trapped in one place and could not refuse to do stunts. La Mesa was too far away for us to have choices anymore.

Ryan and his friends kept us penned up in the various motel rooms, making sure we had just enough food and money for liquor. The motels were too far away from town or the Strip for us to do much else than sit around and eat, drink, and watch television during the day, waiting for their next command. It was too far to walk anywhere, especially in the blazing heat of Vegas in the summer with temperatures upward of 110°, and we had no money for a taxi. Ryan had us exactly where he wanted us.

Every night Ryan would fetch us and take us out for about two to three hours of filming. The Vegas scenes had a whole new element of danger and humiliation. This was no longer an amateur high school video. The stakes were much higher now. With the videos selling and Ryan courting some millionaire Vegas distributors, there was also a new marketing element. Donnie and I had apparently become valuable commodities for Ryan and his friends, who considered themselves businessmen as well as filmmakers.

One of the first scenes shot on this Vegas trip had us dressed in black sweatshirts, "tagging" (with a can of spray paint) homeless people's sleeping bags with "BFK," Ryan's signature "Bum Fight Krew" catchphrase, while they slept. This was very dangerous. We never knew what these homeless guys had stuffed in their sleeping bags. I fully expected someone to pull a gun on me at any moment.

Ryan's solution to this concern was to always have his buddies Tanner and Slyman come along, telling us, "These two guys are your bodyguards." I noticed that although they were young, they seemed pretty tough, like they could hold their own.

Still, when the owners of the sleeping bags being tagged woke up, they were pissed off. Our bodyguards would then step in, but instead of roughing up the homeless guys, they would whip out their wallets and bribe them so as not to cause any trouble.

Donnie and I saw these kinds of dangerous situations as warning signs that we were quickly approaching the point of no return. This hit home when Ryan presented Donnie with a custom-made Vegas-style dare.

"How long do you think it will take you to get kicked out of that casino?" Ryan asked as Bubeck changed the minivideocassette in the camera.

We were lurking in the shadows around the corner from a casino on the high-rent end of the Strip.

Danny Tanner returned from around the corner. "There's this great NASCAR exhibit in there with velvet red ropes and everything," he said, grinning.

"Oh, now you've got to do it, Donnie," Ryan said, laughing.

"What, steal a car or something?" Donnie asked nervously.

"No, nothing like that. Just bust in, duck under the ropes, and climb in a car," Ryan said.

"That sounds stupid. Why do I wanna do that?" Donnie asked.

I looked for a way to blend into the wall, so I wouldn't be chosen if Donnie refused.

"What? Are you afraid or something?" Tanner said, nudging Ryan.

That was all Donnie needed to hear. I sighed in relief; I was off the hook.

"Hell no! I'm not scared!" Donnie exclaimed.

Donnie went into the casino, with Ryan and his camera following close behind. I laughed while I watched Donnie strut through the front doors as if he owned the place. He clearly was trying to get this over with as quickly and painlessly as possible. Ryan nearly had to jog to keep up with him. I hung back, dodging tourist traffic as I watched from the doors.

Donnie marched right over to the crowded exhibit, where dozens of NASCAR fans milled around a precious shrine: a colorful, shiny race car protected only by a circle of red velvet ropes. I couldn't help but think that in any other American city a disheveled, shabbily dressed homeless man with BUMFIGHT tattooed across his forehead might have drawn a few stares as he weaved his way through a tourist attraction. In Vegas, though, nobody batted an eye. That is, until Donnie casually ducked under the rope like he was cutting ahead in line at a theme park. After realizing he was too big to slide in driver-style, Donnie jiggled the door handle. That's when the casino's security guards closed in. They grabbed his arms and escorted him to the front of the casino. As Ryan's film crew moved back toward the door, Tanner checked his watch.

"Four minutes," he shouted to Ryan, and the two exchanged high fives and laughed.

Donnie caught up with me outside. Ryan and the guys had gone to pick up the car. As we watched a bunch of fancy vehicles drive past, Donnie hung his head. I swear for a minute I thought he was about to cry.

"You know, Rufus, I'm beginning to think these guys are a little sick," he muttered as we waited on the curb.

It had barely occurred to me to even ponder this. "I don't know. They give us a place to stay…and booze. You got something better to do besides?" I asked.

Donnie glared at me. "I can't believe you of all people would say this after all the shit they've done to you. Aren't you afraid that one of these times you could get killed or something?"

"Not really. Who'd be their star, then?" I joked. But to tell the truth I really didn't mean it.

The SUV pulled up in front of us.

"I think we should call Barry soon and take him up on his offer to get us home," Donnie said.

I thought about what Donnie had said as we climbed into the car and headed back to the motel. Donnie was worried about our possibly getting killed, but the worst stunts for me were the humiliating ones.

One I clearly remember was wandering around a children's amusement park with rubber dildos strapped to our heads, Ryan and friends following closely behind us, camera rolling as always. Next thing I knew, Donnie and I were crammed side by side into tiny vehicles moving in slow circles in the middle of the amusement park for everyone to see. The dildos were still on our heads, and children surrounded us. I felt so damned humiliated that I just wanted to die.

Somehow there wasn't enough booze in the world to make me so drunk that I wasn't aware of what I was doing. My vision might have been foggy, and I might have been spinning in circles on the kiddie ride, but I still saw the glares of the furious parents and, even worse, the scared, confused looks on the kids' faces. One little girl in particular really got to me. Perched high on her carousel horse, she took one look at me as I staggered by, pointed, and burst into tears. It took everything I had to avoid throwing up right there. I moved as quickly as I could through the crowd—many people laughing along with Ryan and the other filmmakers—and veered around a corner.

"Hey, we didn't yell cut yet, Rufus!" Ryan called out.

I pretended to collapse to the ground, drunker than I really was.

"I think he's down for the count again," Donnie said, coming to my aid.

Ryan bought the excuse and finished filming with Donnie as I leaned against a wall, removing the dildo from my head and hoping I could disappear. That night I started to see Donnie's point about Ryan's being a sick kid. For the first time I felt uneasy about how far this whole *Bumfights* thing was going.

But even if we did decide we wanted out, how the hell were we going to get back to La Mesa?

———

Even while we were starting to have doubts about the films, we had no idea how sick things were about to get for us.

It was Donnie's birthday, August 18, 2002, and Ryan and his friends thought he deserved a special treat. On one of his nightly strolls up the Vegas Strip, looking for filming ideas, Ryan found a treat—two actually. The first hooker's name was Amy, but Ryan apparently had bigger plans for the evening: he needed *two* prostitutes to service Donnie for his birthday. Amy, knowing that she would be unwilling to do some of the things that Ryan had in mind, helped recruit Tonya, who had no qualms about doing anything.

Once Ryan was done with the negotiations, we all went to a cheap motel room for Donnie's birthday celebration. I was drunk enough that I would later forget specific details of the night, which was a blessing. But the video shot that night would serve as one of the more disturbing pieces of evidence in the *Bumfights* court case that lay ahead for Ryan and his fellow filmmakers. And the sadistic things that went down that night would come back to haunt me like an out-of-focus nightmare.

Through a drunken haze I watched my even-more-inebriated friend strip naked at Ryan's command. Ryan and the others were in the corner of the room, shouting constant instructions. I saw one hooker push Donnie onto the bed and shove a blue rubber ball into his mouth, while the filmmakers shouted instructions to her in between their whooping and hollering. I vaguely remember watching her give Donnie a blow job.

"Rufus, why don't you go help her?" Ryan yelled over the raucous cheers.

Too drunk to speak, all I could do was glance at Ryan and grunt.

"Dude, what are you saying?" Zach Bubeck yelled, exploding in laughter.

"Nah, man, that's not what I meant...Hey, bitch, take this and start whipping him," Ryan said, shoving a sturdy riding crop into Tonya's hands. He had brought it along for just such a scene.

Tonya did as she was told, hitting Donnie hard in the testicles with the rigid metal rod, turning them red and swollen almost instantly.

"Hit him in the balls harder! Harder!" Ryan yelled.

Tonya obeyed. As the camera rolled, Donnie bellowed so loud it shook my bones.

"Come on, Rufus. Go help her out! Donnie needs his birthday spanking!" Ryan instructed, pushing me toward the bed as the laughter reached fever pitch.

I did as I was told, whipping and spanking Donnie as the camera kept rolling. Some Vegas cops showed up at one point, responding to Donnie's screams and the shouts of the raucous filmmakers, but there were no reports or arrests. I may have been bleary-eyed, but I swear one of the cops winked at Ryan as he walked out the door. For all I know, Ryan might've slipped the cop some cash. He had gotten so good at showing outsiders his side of the story—and sometimes sweetening the pot—that I began to wonder exactly how much these guys would get away with before this thing was over. Fortunately, Donnie finally passed out cold, and that's what ended his birthday "celebration."

The following day, waking up in serious pain, Donnie remembered what had happened to him. The lower part of his body hurt so much that he couldn't even stand up. The horrific images from the previous night started flashing back to haunt me too. We no longer had any doubt: we needed to get the hell away from Ryan and his cronies. The problem was, at this point, we were basically being held captive, with no money or means of escaping.

Ryan had put us up in a two-bedroom apartment this time, again on the outskirts of the city. But we weren't alone. When we first arrived at the apartment, Ryan had said, "I know this homeless guy. Is it okay if he stays here with you guys?"

The guy's name was James, and I guessed he was in his early twenties—old enough to go to the liquor store and buy booze for us anyway. What we found odd was that James was clean and neatly dressed. We knew what homeless folks looked like, and there was nothing about this guy that said "homeless."

It turned out that James was a friend of Ryan's, and he had been planted at the apartment to keep an eye on us and make sure we didn't go anywhere. He was our "prison guard." Ryan had invested a lot of money in his circus animals, and he wanted to make sure we didn't break out of the cage. For Donnie and me this meant making sure the booze supply was always ample. We were more addicted and bored than ever, being cooped up in the apartment most of the time with no means of escaping. If James got us fifty beers, we'd soon send him out for fifty more. I wasn't sure if this was considered hitting rock bottom, but damn, it sure felt like it—sitting around drinking all day and getting humiliated and battered at night.

At one point Ryan's girlfriend, Cara, told Donnie what both of us already knew: "All Ryan is doing is just using you."

Donnie replied, "Sure he is," and I agreed. But with no money or transportation, and James watching us like a hawk, we didn't know how to get out of the increasingly bad situation. We needed money, and I was starting to come up with an idea of how we could get it.

———

From Ryan McPherson's first conversation about *Bumfights* with Donnie and me, he had promised to include us in all the fortunes bound to come from the video series. After all, we were the stars of the movie.

During our final stay in Vegas, Donnie and I were surprised at how many people on the Strip recognized us. I suddenly remembered all those posters with my face on them, decorating the walls of Ryan's apartment and finally made the connection. Ryan must already be selling the videos.

Once I realized that, I wondered when the money Ryan had been constantly promising us would start rolling in. The only compensation we received continued to be a place to stay, lots of booze—more of a way of getting through the stunts than anything—and food. After a couple of dozen people had stopped us for photos, yelled at us, and even cussed us out, I figured that Ryan had to be selling a lot of videos for all these people to know who the hell we were.

Late in the summer of 2002, we finally got a taste of exactly what kind of dough the kid had been talking about for the past three years when we all met with Ryan's attorney to sign the official release form. The release promised a direct bank deposit of forty thousand dollars to me and ten thousand dollars for Donnie—I guess doing more stunts and spilling more blood was worth four times as much. Looking at those numbers, I suddenly realized that if Ryan was promising that kind of money to us, a couple of bums, then he and the other film-makers (including the new Vegas investors to whom they had recently sold the film rights) must really be cleaning up. Naturally we didn't get a dime that day—or any other day—and we were so drunk that I don't even remember signing the damned papers.

I also figured that if our stunts were so profitable, Ryan likely wouldn't be losing interest in us anytime soon.

Finally I wasn't willing to sit around and wait for things to get any worse. Later that night, after we were locked up in the apartment, James went out to the liquor store. Then I confronted Donnie about our situation.

"Donnie, you know all that money in those forms today…That's like they put bounties on us. They're never going to let us leave if the shit we're doing is worth that much, ya know."

"I'm glad you're starting to see my point, but what the hell do we do about it?" Donnie asked.

"Barry told us, if you ever wanna come back, I'll get you back, and I'll put you up in a place in La Mesa," I said.

"You think the guy will come?"

"Shit, I hope so."

"I don't know, man. You think it'll work? What if we get caught? We've seen what happens when Ryan gets pissed."

"Donnie, I know in my heart that these fuckers are never going to take us back to La Mesa. They'll keep us here as long as they want. And who knows what'll happen then? Besides, you're the one who got me thinkin' about all this. You ready to get the hell out of here? Let's go now! Let's just get our clothes and friggin' leave."

Donnie nodded. "Yeah, okay, call him. But we'd better wait till he gets here before we do anything."

I dug out Barry's number, picked up the house phone, and prepared to make the call.

CHAPTER 10
JEWISH JAMES BONDS

BARRY SOPER WOULD EVENTUALLY FILL ME IN ABOUT everything that was happening on his end prior to and after I called him. By this time the La Mesa Police were more informed about the *Bumfights* videos than they had been when Ryan and the rest of us initially fled to Vegas. They had contacted the district attorney's office, and as Ryan had feared, the district attorney had launched a full-fledged investigation.

Since Donnie and I had worked for Barry, the DA made a paper connection between us. About the time that Donnie was getting his birthday spanking from the Vegas prostitute, the DA had called to ask Barry if he knew where the "bums" were. Barry told them that he did not—at least he didn't have to lie to them at that point. The DA's office then revealed how they suspected that, based on information they had gathered during their investigation, Ryan had taken Donnie and me to Las Vegas.

The DA's office also told Barry that they had launched a criminal investigation into these filmmakers and that if he did find us, to be careful and call the police—either in La Mesa or Las Vegas, as both departments were now on the hunt for Ryan McPherson and his

friends. They even suspected that the new distributors to whom Ryan
had sold the film rights were tied to the Vegas mob.

After Barry received that disturbing information from the DA's
office, we made the call from Las Vegas and gave him the address of
the apartment. Barry told us to stay put, that he would get there as
soon as he could.

But in his mind Barry had to wonder just what the hell he was
getting into. The Vegas *mob*? Visions of Don Vito Corleone spun
around in his head. Was he going to risk his life for a couple of homeless guys who had once raided his Dumpster?

But how could he *not* help them, he thought, as he called his
cousin and good friend, Barry Plotkin, an attorney who happened to
be in Las Vegas at a conference. "Rufus sounded frantic, BP," he said,
using his cousin's nickname. "He told me that the stunts were getting
more dangerous, things like setting homeless men's hair on fire and
pulling out their own teeth with pliers."

"Are you shitting me?" BP exclaimed.

"He even said something about a...snuff film."

"Oh, for crying out loud, Sopy! You can't—"

Barry interrupted and said to pick him up at the airport in a few
hours. Then he called his daughter, Jill, who now lived in Las Vegas.
Jill did some speedy detective work and confirmed that someone—
James—was almost always watching the apartment. At that point
Barry had no idea how he was going to get us away from the apart-
ment or even what he was going to do when he got there. But that
did not stop him from hopping the next Southwest Airlines flight to
Las Vegas.

Once he was there, his cousin drove him to the Mirage Hotel,
where they started plotting together. "It was kind of comical really,"

Barry told me later. "Here you have two middle-aged nerds, suddenly pretending to be Jewish James Bonds, trying to bust some homeless guys out of a guarded apartment on the outskirts of Sin City!"

They finally mustered enough courage to go through with their master plan. As they drove to the apartment building, BP complained of stomach pains the entire way and begged Barry to reconsider.

"This is absolutely nuts, Sopy," BP groaned as he intentionally drove slowly enough to catch every red light en route.

"Come on. Drive faster. And it's not nuts. I made a promise to Rufus and Donnie, and I intend to keep it."

"They're frigging drunks! You think they're going to remember?" BP asked.

"Maybe not, but *I'll* remember," he said.

They arrived at the apartment complex, which they noticed was a heck of a lot nicer than what they'd expected. BP stayed outside with the engine running. Barry walked around the back of the building, found the unit, knocked on the door, and quickly scurried around the side of the building to hide. If James was there, Barry didn't know what he would do. Ever since he'd heard the word *mob* connected with the guys holding us hostage, he was driven by sheer terror to get us out of Vegas and back to La Mesa as quickly as possible. He peered around the corner of the building and was relieved when Donnie came walking out. James had left to pick up some food.

I was sitting in the living room, drinking a beer and watching television, when Barry burst in. "Come on! I'm getting you guys out of here!" he exclaimed.

It was already late in the afternoon, and I was so drunk that it took a few moments for me to absorb this. I noticed Barry sweating and was afraid he might keel over from a heart attack.

Donnie and I looked at each other and nodded. We knew this would be our only chance to get out of the Bum Fight Krew. Hell, this was what we wanted. Barry helped us gather our stuff so we could get out of there fast before James came back. He was convinced that this could happen at any moment, based on the action movie playing in his head.

Finally he ran around the corner of the building with the two of us struggling to keep up. His cousin's eyes grew wide with panic when he saw us. "Are you kidding me, Sopy?" he yelled.

Donnie and I looked at him in surprise. Considering how we must've smelled, the guy was lucky he wasn't standing downwind of us.

"Just get in the car, guys," Barry told us, anxiously glancing around the parking lot.

We tossed our belongings into the backseat and climbed in, and now the smell hit Barry's cousin.

"Jeez, we're going to get our asses killed." BP gagged, refusing to leave with us in his car.

"Don't be a schmuck. Let's get out of here!" Barry snapped forcefully enough that BP put the car in gear and sped out of the parking lot.

In the backseat, Donnie and I glanced at each other nervously. These scrawny nerds were coming to our rescue? It seemed unlikely that we would be able to avert disaster.

"Now what the hell do we do with them?" BP asked Barry, as if referring to some stray dogs they had picked up.

It didn't appear as if these two guys had any kind of an exit strategy for getting us out of Vegas. Barry might have thought of them as Jewish James Bonds, but at that moment, he told me later on, he felt more like the bumbling Inspector Clouseau.

"All right. Just get us to the airport," he finally told BP. "I'll put us all on the first flight to San Diego." He turned and looked at us. "You have your IDs, don't you?"

"Yeah, I do," I said, but Donnie shook his head as he dug in his pockets.

"Uh, must've left it at the apartment. Can we go—"

"Hell no, we're not going back!" BP snapped. "Okay, Sopy, what now? You can't get them through security."

"Besides," I added, "I ain't never been up in a plane, and I ain't about to start now."

With Barry's cousin close to a coronary, Donnie decided to take matters into his own hands. "Just drop us at the Greyhound terminal. Rufus and I will see you in San Diego," he said.

"Yeah, don't worry about us," I added.

"Great idea," BP said, and he sped off toward the bus station. When we got there, Barry forked over three hundred dollars and put us on a bus to La Mesa, telling us to call him as soon as we arrived. I know he was hoping that we wouldn't spend the money on booze and gambling. I later told him that we were tempted, but we managed to buy the bus tickets after they left us. He also had us sign a retainer agreement for a law firm that he intended to hire to help us with any future litigation.

Although Barry never did have a run-in with any Vegas-mob film-makers, he was still a wreck, he later told me. For a mild-mannered businessman, this was quite an adventure. He had thought about calling the Vegas police when he arrived, but then he decided, what the hell? You only live once. Go for it. Save the guys.

For Donnie and me this rescue was the miracle we had been hoping for. By the end of the day we sat on a bus headed back home.

———

Soon after returning to La Mesa, we called Barry from a Mobil station in a panic. We figured that we were coming back home to pick up where we left off, hopefully with fewer police hassles. But when we returned, it wasn't the police hassling us—it was the media. They were asking us about a lawsuit and about Ryan's being in jail. We didn't know what the hell these goddamned reporters were talking about.

We soon found out from Barry that, in the days surrounding our big escape, Ryan McPherson had been arrested in La Mesa at his parents' home. While Donnie and I were leaving Las Vegas, the kid who'd been holding us captive there was in jail himself. At first we didn't know if he'd returned to Southern California before we left, or if he'd do that afterward, maybe to track us down and try to bring us back. We found out afterward that he'd been arrested back home two days before Barry had sprung us. In any case there was no way we would be working with him again. Our acting careers were over.

None of us knew it as yet, but the story of the bums who had fought and the filmmakers who'd caught it on tape was about to make its way well beyond La Mesa, California, and Las Vegas, Nevada. After our homecoming we thought all this was behind us. But it had hardly begun.

PART 4

GETTING STRAIGHT

CHAPTER 11

A SOBERING HOMECOMING

ON WEDNESDAY, SEPTEMBER 25, 2002, AT THE EL CAJON courthouse in the East County Regional Center, Deputy District Attorney Curtis Ross arraigned *Bumfights* producers Ryan McPherson, Daniel Tanner, Zachary Bubeck, and Michael Slyman. The charges entailed crimes against two homeless men: Rufus Hannah and Donnie Brennan. Later on I would have a chance to hear the official felony charges at one of the many meetings with the lawyers whom Barry had retained for Donnie and me. The charges were soliciting someone to commit a felony (assault with a deadly weapon), inflicting serious bodily injury, conspiracy to commit a crime, and the misdemeanor of staging an illegal fight for money. The defendants were represented by a team of some of San Diego's best (according to Barry) defense attorneys: Jan Ronis, Michael Pancer, and Patrick Hall.

———

Prior to all this arraignment business Donnie and I were happy to be back behind the Mobil station in La Mesa that we called home, and we were even more pleased to have some money in our pockets. "Hey, you know that we still have a bunch of Barry's dough. Let's get some drinks and food," I said, trying not to think about the ton of money we had never gotten from Ryan or his attorneys.

"Hell yeah," Donnie replied.

I breathed a sigh of relief. Maybe things were going to return to normal after all. I sure as hell hoped that everything relevant to *Bumfights* was done and over with forever, and that I'd never hear Ryan McPherson's name again.

On the morning before the arraignment Donnie and I were passed out drunk in the back parking lot of the gas station where we had been living before Ryan took us to Sin City. By this time we had spent nearly all of Barry's money. I kept dreaming about a swarm of bees chasing me, their continuous buzzing getting closer and closer until...

My eyes snapped open. I looked up, but instead of insects swarming, I saw reporters closing in with whirring cameras and tape recorders. I quickly elbowed Donnie awake.

"Wha' the fuck..." My friend groaned.

"I think we gotta get up," I grumbled.

Donnie looked around in bewilderment as we helped each other up and grasped our duffel bags protectively. No sooner had we risen than an explosion of light and voices erupted from all directions.

"Are you Rufus and Donnie?" a voice shouted.

"I think that's them," another one cut in before either of us could respond.

"What was your involvement in the *Bumfights* videos?" someone said loudly.

"How do you know Ryan McPherson?" a woman chirped as she tried to elbow her way to the front, pushing a small tape recorder in Donnie's face.

Donnie shoved the device away, and we started pushing through the crowd toward a pay phone to call Barry Soper. Undeterred, the media swarm persisted. I glared in disgust at all the camera lenses pointed toward me. I'd already had enough of being on camera to last a couple of lifetimes.

"Can you comment on the arrests of Ryan McPherson and the others behind the *Bumfights* videos?" the chirpy woman continued.

That got me out of my drunken stupor. "Ryan's in jail?" I blurted.

We had finally made it to the pay phone, where I fished through my bag for change.

"Yes," the reporter said, handing me some coins. "Do you have any comments?"

"We just wanna be left the hell alone," Donnie grumbled.

"I understand that, but if you could just answer a few questions for us?"

A new bunch of antenna-topped vans pulled into the gas station. It was as if they were breeding.

"Give us a minute, will you?" I snapped and shooed the swarm away as I put the coins in and dialed.

The media backed off a few feet and consulted with one another, some talking on cell phones, all the while keeping a collective eye on us, making sure their lead story didn't get away. I was sick of being told what to do, of being someone else's property. Donnie felt the same way. He lit up a cigarette and blew smoke as hard as he could at the reporters, trying to create a wall between them and us. It worked on the woman. She backed up a few more feet, coughing and waving her hand in front of her face.

Barry answered the phone, and I said, "We've got a big problem, Barry."

"What is it?" Barry asked.

"There's fuckin' media and camera crews all over us. What do we do?"

The swarm was starting to inch closer, so Donnie let out a loud, rasping cough, driving them back again.

"Don't say a word," Barry told us. "I'm over at the Lakewood Villa Townhomes and will be there in a few minutes."

"What are we supposed to do? They keep trying to get us to talk to them." I knew I sounded anxious.

"I'm serious, Rufus. Don't say a word—I'm on my way," Barry said.

"Okay." I hung up and told Donnie, "We're not supposed to say a word."

We looked at the growing swarm of media. "Now how the hell are we supposed to do that?" Donnie snapped.

We walked quickly away from the reporters and back behind the building. The swarm followed.

"Leave us the hell alone. We got nothing to say to you!" Donnie bellowed, and they again backed off.

The reporters watched us settle back into our usual spots, smoke some cigarettes, and generally stare into space. Finally coming to the realization that we weren't the best interview subjects, the media retreated to the edge of the parking lot to hatch a new plan of action.

While we were alone for the moment, we felt safe enough to start a whispered conversation.

"What the hell do you think they're talking about, with Ryan going to jail?" I said.

"Beats me. Maybe this is all a stunt, and Ryan's trying to set us up again," Donnie suggested.

"You think?" I stared at all the television cameras and wondered if Donnie was right. Maybe this was the most elaborate, extensively filmed scene for the videos so far. "I hope you're wrong. I can't take any more of that shit."

A few minutes later Barry pulled around to the back of the lot. We grabbed our backpacks and got in his car quickly as the reporters continued yelling.

"What is your connection to Rufus and Donnie?" The same woman reporter attempted to shove her tape recorder into Barry's face.

"They have no comment. We'll get back to you," Barry said, waving them away.

He drove slowly through the thickening crowd of news vans and reporters and finally reached the street. "Some of those news crews," he said, "are down from Los Angeles, and—good God, there's ABC! *Good Morning America*, which is national. I think this is going to get a whole lot bigger."

I couldn't process that, so instead I asked, "Where are we going?"

"Somewhere safe...I've got to catch you guys up on a few things," Barry said as he pulled onto the freeway.

"Yeah, what's this about Ryan going to jail?" Donnie asked.

"That's right. The Deputy District Attorney, Curtis Ross, filed criminal charges against McPherson, Bubeck, Tanner, and Slyman."

I grinned. "Does that mean they're all locked up now?"

"They were arrested and put in jail briefly, but no, they're out now. There are two criminal complaints pending against them, a felony, and some misdemeanors. That's why all the media was after you guys back there."

"How did Ryan like being arrested?" I asked, thinking that our being kept in that Vegas apartment all day had also been like being in jail.

"Not too much, apparently. I heard from the police that he kept saying how he didn't do anything wrong. The arresting officer asked him if he knew where you guys were, and Ryan said, 'I don't have to tell you that.' He had an ATM slip on him when they arrested him."

"Yeah, how much did that bastard make off of us?" Donnie asked.

"The balance said $285,000—and that was just his checking account."

"Son of a bitch!" I exclaimed. "All that dough and we got nothing— even after we signed all of his damn papers!"

"When he was in the San Diego County Jail, they said he was crying and shaking and telling everyone that as soon as he got out he was going to Mexico and never coming back," Barry added.

"If they ever put him back in, I hope they never let him out," Donnie said.

"Unfortunately it doesn't work that way, Donnie."

I snorted in disgust as Donnie looked out the window. We were getting closer to the coast. I inhaled deeply as the salty air drifted through my window in the backseat. All I wanted was to forget about the pain and humiliation of the *Bumfights*, but Barry seemed determined to make me keep remembering. I felt tired and hungry, and my body ached for alcohol. I just wanted to be left alone, but I guess we needed to know what he was telling us.

Barry continued, "So anyway, Rufus, right after you called me this morning I got on the phone with an attorney friend of mine, Browne Greene, up in Santa Monica. He's part of a big law firm up there: Greene, Broillet, Panish and Wheeler."

"Aren't they the guys on those papers we signed after you picked us up in Vegas?" Donnie asked.

"Yeah, the retainer agreement. Anyway, Browne told me, 'Barry, you get those guys the hell out of here and put them in a motel.' I'm taking you to an E-Z 8 Motel in San Diego at the edge of Old Town. I called on the way. They're expecting us."

We spent the rest of the drive catching up on everything else that had been happening. Donnie and I filled Barry in on many of the details of our time in Las Vegas. Throughout all the stories—from the dildos at the amusement park to the prostitutes on Donnie's birthday—Barry grew angrier and angrier, swearing at Ryan and the others.

"That's awful! That's just really awful," he finally concluded.

"We didn't have a choice," I said defensively.

"I'm not blaming you. It's awful that those jerks would take advantage of you like that."

"But they'll go to jail, right?" Donnie asked, a hopeful look on his face.

"I hope so. Browne Greene is a great lawyer, and I know he's going to work really hard for you guys in the civil case," Barry said as we pulled into the motel parking lot. My brain still being foggy, I didn't get much of what he was saying about any case, and I didn't really care. I just wanted to get some sleep.

Old Town is the most historic and most visited area of San Diego. There are plenty of trolleys and buses for easy transportation, and I immediately noticed the liquor store across the street. Barry drove us right up to the motel office in the center of a square courtyard.

"Home sweet home," he announced and then checked us into a standard room, paying the manager for a week and putting the room in his name. "Great, another motel room to be cooped up in," I grumbled as he helped us settle in.

"Would you rather go back to the Vons or the Mobil?" Barry asked.

"No," Donnie said firmly, adding, "Shut up, Rufus."

I plopped down on the bed, flicked on the television, and ignored them. Barry handed the room key to Donnie.

"Are you guys hungry?" he asked.

"Yeah," Donnie replied as I turned up the volume.

Everything Barry said and did was pissing me off more and more. I didn't see the difference between Ryan's confining Donnie and me to a motel to do what he wanted—the videos—and Barry doing the same thing for his own reason—this lawsuit he was babbling on about. I wanted to be left alone more than ever, but the whole damn world kept closing in on me.

"Come on, Rufus. Barry's taking us out for some food." Donnie kicked the bed.

I stood with a sour look on my face and followed them to Barry's car. The prospect of food and a free room had made Donnie all cheerful and talkative again. He chatted animatedly with Barry as he drove, even telling jokes. I watched from the backseat as Barry apparently ate up the Donnie Show with a spoon. I snickered under my breath, thinking, *Donnie sure knows how to work it, and this guy is getting worked.* Although it did occur to me that, without Donnie, Barry might never have given me the time of day. So I decided to keep my big mouth shut around him from then on so I wouldn't say anything that might get Donnie and me in trouble.

After buying a fast-food lunch, Barry took us to a market for groceries and a carton of Marlboros. He made us promise not to get drunk or talk to the press under any circumstances. The first request was wishful thinking; he probably knew that.

We returned to the motel room. "You guys all set now?" Barry said from the doorway.

"Can we get some money for doing our laundry?" Donnie asked.

Barry handed Donnie a couple of dollars. Then he looked at me, once again back on the bed and flipping through television channels, ignoring him as usual. Barry sighed and walked to his car. I looked out the window to make sure he was leaving.

"What's your problem, man?" Donnie said.

"I don't trust this guy," I said.

Donnie shrugged. "You're the one who said to call him and get us out of Vegas."

"Well, I trusted those other guys less than him."

"So what are we supposed to do, then?"

I thought for a minute, continuing to flip through the channels. "I'll tell you one thing: we gotta find some booze. What the hell was he trying to prove, not even buying us a beer?"

"How're we gonna buy booze if we don't have enough money?" Donnie held up the measly two dollars Barry had left.

I thought for another minute and then pointed to the cigarettes. "He doesn't seem to have a problem buying us smokes. Let's see if we can sell 'em out on the street."

A lightbulb went off in Donnie's head. "Now you're talking!"

—

Almost immediately after setting us up in the motel room, Barry created a makeshift meal-delivery program with the help of his son, Blair, who was attending law school at the University of San Diego. One of them would drive over three times a day to deliver fast-food meals to Donnie and me. Each delivery went basically the same way. Barry would enter the smoke-filled room—more like a gas chamber, he said—and drop off the food with barely a word in return from Donnie and nothing at all from me. There were also the increasingly regular Marlboro deliveries that, unknown to them, had become valuable bartering tools for us to trade for booze.

Barry repeatedly told us not to associate with any of our old friends and said that absolutely no overnight guests were allowed in the room that he was paying for. Unfortunately old habits refused to die, and the homeless population of La Mesa made its way over to the E-Z 8 to see Donnie and me.

Crankshaft, Donnie's fellow Vietnam vet, was known for his wartime job on "rat patrol." It was called this for two reasons: the extremely narrow tunnels were breeding grounds for snakes and rats, and also because the Vietcong would hide there, popping up in strategic areas to attack the American forces. He made a point of reminding anyone who would listen about how it was one of the worst jobs imaginable. Almost every trip into the tunnels would result in many American troops being killed. Crankshaft was frequently called upon for rat duty because he was thin and could fit through the narrow openings that led into the tunnels.

Then there was freaking Steve Boyd, a veteran who claimed to be homeless by choice due to spending his every dime to send his daughter to Stanford. He claimed that his wife was in Canada. He claimed a lot of things, most of them figments of his imagination. One thing that particularly irritated me about Steve was the puppy he would bring with him to the already cramped motel room. The idiot dog barked and kept me up all night. It also crapped on the carpet.

It seemed that the small motel room had turned into a magnet for every friend, vet, pet, and family member in the greater San Diego area—and the room had the smell to prove it. There were four guys in the room at any given time, and more often there were at least six to eight guys crammed in. Donnie and I had our own beds, and the other guys laid out sleeping bags on the floor.

Every time Barry walked through the door, the overwhelming stench of smoke, body odor, rotted food, and booze hit him smack in the face. He gave us some leniency for breaking the rules, probably because he was feeling sorry for us. But one day the situation finally came to a head.

"Rufus, Donnie, can I see you guys outside for a minute?" Barry yelled through the smoky haze and crowd of yet more homeless people who filled the room.

We went outside, and Donnie asked, "What's up?"

"Listen, I've been feeding you guys, giving you laundry money, buying you cartons of cigarettes and groceries, and paying for your room. *Please* do me a favor in return and try to drink less and smoke outside."

"That it?" I said.

"And no more of your homeless friends in your room," he added.

"First of all this is a smoking room. Check the back of the door, man. You can't tell us not to smoke," I said.

"I'm not telling you. I'm asking you—man-to-man."

"Fuck you," I said and started to go back inside.

"I thought I'd asked you to give up the booze before the trial," he said.

I slammed the door behind me.

"How do you know we haven't?" Donnie said.

Barry flailed his arms in disgust. "Give me a break. There are a lot of smells coming out of that room, but I can still tell that the booze smell is coming off you guys like vapors."

Donnie glared at him and went back into the room. Barry shook his head and walked back to his car.

His next visit to the E-Z 8 pissed him off even more. He knocked on the door to pick us up for lunch. Donnie came out almost immediately. I watched from inside the room.

"Hi, Barry," Donnie said casually.

"Hi, Do—"

Before he could finish, Donnie whipped out his dick and started peeing on the ground.

Barry was stunned. "What the hell do you think you're doing?"

"What's the matter, Barry? The great outdoors is part of my domain," Donnie said.

"Like hell it is!" he exclaimed. "What are you trying to do, get me arrested with you for indecent exposure? The bathroom is just a couple of feet away in your room. What's the matter with you?"

Inside the motel room I laughed my ass off.

The next time Barry returned to try to make a more convincing case for us to stop drinking and clean up our acts, he brought help. I glanced up from the television as he walked in with a fine-looking woman. "Guys, I'd like to introduce my dear friend Carrie Snodgress. She's an actress who came all the way down from Hollywood to talk to you," he said, smiling.

Carrie sat down on the bed across from me and started to talk. I noticed how she looked both of us in the eye when she spoke and really seemed like she cared about what happened to us. For a moment my hatred and distrust of Barry lifted, maybe because a lady like this was willing to be friends with a guy like him.

Barry told us how he'd met Carrie when he was on the board of directors for Oak Grove, a residential treatment center for behavioral problems and child abuse. Carrie was best known for a movie called *Diary of a Mad Housewife*, for which she was nominated for the best actress Oscar. She'd also been music legend Neil Young's girlfriend, and they had a child together. Young's hit song "Heart of Gold" was written for Carrie.

One day over lunch Barry had told her about Donnie and me. She told Barry that she would like to come down to San Diego and talk to us. Carrie had been through recovery for alcoholism, and she indeed was a woman with a heart of gold.

Soon she got down to business. Carrie talked to Donnie and me about how we were throwing our lives away with alcohol. She told us how upset it made her that we were taking advantage of her "dear friend Barry." (I fought the urge to roll my eyes because of how upset she seemed about that.) She even said how she would assist in getting us into a rehab program to help us "get the monkeys" off our backs.

"You are both acting like you're dying, but you have to live now. It is up to you to do this, one day at a time," she told us.

"I will!" I blurted out before I could stop myself.

All eyes in the room turned to me. Barry's jaw dropped. Carrie smiled gently at me.

"Good," she said and then left.

A couple of years later Barry told me how that sweet lady died a painful death from liver failure. I couldn't help but remember how she went out of her way that day for a rude drunk like me with the slim hope that something she said to me would make a difference. On that day it didn't make much of a dent in my outlook on life—although ultimately it would.

Barry planned to pay for us to stay at the motel for quite some time while the *Bumfights* lawsuits played out. His main reason was to protect us from the media. The other was to keep us as sober as possible and in one place, where he and the attorneys could find us for important meetings and legal dates.

We knew this, but it didn't stop us from going out at night and bartering for the cash we needed for booze, hanging out with our friends, and basically doing whatever the hell we wanted. Most of the time we managed to be back in the room when he came to pick us up for appointments.

Barry had been right regarding what he'd said about the media on the day he rescued us from all those reporters. By now every media outlet in the world was fighting for an exclusive scoop on the two La Mesa homeless guys who had been taken advantage of by the cocky rich kids. While Donnie and I lay low at the E-Z 8, our team of attorneys and publicists fielded interview and information requests from every newspaper, magazine, and talk show across the globe.

Damned if the perfect media storm hadn't begun to form in downtown San Diego. Ready or not—like it or not—our time had come to face a hell of a lot of public scrutiny during the lawsuits. To tell the truth I didn't know if I was up for it.

CHAPTER 12
FUNERAL PARLORS

OUR PART OF THE *BUMFIGHTS* LAWSUITS OFFICIALLY BEGAN on Tuesday, October 1, 2002, in the San Diego office of Barry Plotkin, attorney at law. The meeting was scheduled for 9 a.m. and would include Donnie, me, our attorneys, Browne Greene and Mark Quigley, our publicist, Kathy Pinckert, and Barry Soper. Kathy was the marketing and media relations person for the law firm. Barry and the rest had no doubt that she'd be kept busy.

Barry picked us up at the motel early that morning and took us across the street for breakfast. Looking us up and down, he sniffed the air as we walked to the car.

"What?" Donnie asked.

"You guys are actually sober. I'm pleasantly surprised," he said.

"You only told us to be sober about a hundred times when you dropped us off after dinner last night," I muttered with obvious sarcasm.

At the diner Donnie dug into a trucker's special. I just sipped coffee, trying to calm my nerves and my hands. I also worked hard to avoid Barry's suspicious gaze across the table. I figured that he could see through me, and I knew that if we made eye contact, I might say something to jeopardize the free food and cigarettes. A particularly big tremor suddenly overtook my hands, and I struggled with the coffee mug.

"Is he okay?" Barry asked Donnie.

This was pretty much the communication system from the time he had checked us into the motel. When it was absolutely necessary, he would communicate with me through Donnie, my interpreter. This only made me hate the guy even more.

"Yup, he's good," Donnie said, barely looking up between mouthfuls of scrambled eggs and toast.

"You guys swear you did what I said and didn't drink last night, right?" Barry asked suspiciously.

We sneaked guilty glances at each other across the table. Neither of us would admit that we hadn't drank, and this was the exact reason we were jittery. We were both going through withdrawal tremors right in front of him. Even if we had wanted to drink last night, we'd run out of laundry money and cigarettes to barter with. We had no way to buy any booze.

"We need another carton of cigarettes before you take off today, Barry," Donnie said.

"Another one?" he exclaimed. "Blair just got you a carton a few days ago. I didn't know you guys were such chain-smokers."

"Yeah, well, I picked it up in the army. Rufus—well, I think he picked it up when he was in elementary school," Donnie said, trying to laugh off my concern.

Barry looked at his watch and grabbed the check off the table. "Time to go. We don't want to be late."

—

Donnie and I, our legal team, and Barry gathered around a giant table in a vast conference room at Barry Plotkin's law office. Browne

Greene, the lead attorney, stood and told us about his prestigious Santa Monica law firm. Tall and strong in stature, he wore a real fine suit, but I couldn't get past the older guy's funny little bow tie. He reminded me of a carnival barker.

Greene explained how the civil case against Ryan and his friends was going to be filed the next day and that there was going to be a press conference outside the San Diego courthouse. My head started to swim as he went on and on. Next Greene told us how some television news show called *The Abrams Report* or something, plus a bunch of others, was going to interview us after that. I wondered if the annoying lady reporter from the gas station would be there. Then I wondered why I wasn't supposed to talk to them before, but now it was okay. All the lawyers' chatter, combined with a whole day without alcohol, was making me feel sick, tired, and dizzy.

"Rufus, Browne asked you a question," Barry said, nudging me lightly on the arm.

As I turned to look at him, everything went black.

—*—

When I finally opened my eyes and gazed around—still through a foggy veil—the room was silent, and everyone was looking down at me anxiously. The publicist rubbed my neck and back.

"What the hell just happened?" I mumbled.

"You had a seizure and fell out of your chair," Barry said.

"Sorry," I mumbled and tried to sit up.

"It's okay, Rufus," Greene said. "We were just about done anyway. Make sure you get some food and plenty of sleep for the big day tomorrow."

Barry brought us back to the motel after stopping to buy a carton of cigarettes on the way. Once back at the motel, however, instead of just dropping us off, he followed us into the room. He was bound and determined to hang around as long as possible to make sure that whatever mysterious source caused my seizure wouldn't happen again. I felt sure that if the seizure had come from alcohol withdrawal, I was on my way to an even bigger one. If it had come from something else…Well, hell, I wasn't interested in trying to figure that one out. My main interest now was getting Barry the hell out the door so Donnie and I could get on the streets and start selling our new smokes for booze money.

Barry finally left after sundown. We immediately hit the streets. We weren't able to sell all the packs, but our efforts did get us a six-pack of beer, which calmed my nerves a bit.

By 8:30 the next morning we were all back in the law office, discussing last-minute strategy. I felt sick again, and my head ached. I was anxious for this whole thing to be over with so Donnie and I could go back home to La Mesa and resume our lives.

The bow-tied lawyer stood up again and started talking about what we were supposed to say at the press conference. "I'm going to talk first," he said. "Then I will introduce Barry, and he'll tell how he met you guys and then how he retained our services. Donnie, then you'll tell how you were victimized by the defendants—"

"Who?" Donnie asked.

"Ryan, Bubeck, and the others," Barry explained.

"Okay?" Greene asked.

"Yeah," Donnie said.

"Then, Rufus, you'll finish up the interview by telling your story." Everyone looked at me. They probably wondered if I'd pass out again.

"How are you doing, Rufus?" Greene finally asked me.

I looked up at him, and damn, everything went black again.

—··—

This time I didn't wake up right away, and everything wasn't back to normal again so soon with just food and rest.

I woke up in Donald J. Sharp Memorial Hospital and was told that I'd had a grand mal seizure—the most serious kind. Seizures such as these, not to mention heart attacks and strokes, can all occur during alcohol withdrawal—even in the little bit of time that I'd been without a drink while preparing to talk to the lawyers. I also weighed an unhealthy 110 pounds.

After the doctors and nurses stabilized me, I settled back in the bed and turned on the television. I immediately saw some familiar faces: the press conference outside the San Diego courthouse was in progress.

A podium had been set up on the steps, and the press was already gathered and waiting. They were eager to hear the personal stories from the two homeless men themselves: the now-famous bums of the *Bumfights* videos. They all watched as Browne Greene approached the podium. He described the "outrageous acts committed by the defendants against these two helpless home-less men." He detailed the allegations in the civil complaints, the damages we were requesting, and described the severity of the injuries we had sustained.

"Rufus and Donnie were human billboards for the *Bumfights*," he continued. "The defendants made over six million dollars, and Rufus and Donnie only received money for beer. They were maimed and branded with tattoos like Holocaust victims and permanently injured in many other ways. The real bums are the ones behind the camera, not the ones in front of the camera."

Resting in my hospital bed, I was pleased that at least someone understood the shit Donnie and I had been through.

"How do you respond to comments by the defendants that the plaintiffs gave their consent to appear in the videos in exchange for alcohol and small amounts of money?" a reporter asked.

"You don't have consent when you deliberately intoxicate someone," said Mark Quigley.

Barry stepped up and further painted the picture behind the lawsuit, describing how he had met Donnie and me before we were in the videos. He described the two hardworking homeless men who showed up sober every day for many weeks, wanting nothing more than to make an honest living.

The media was disappointed when Browne Greene announced that I would not be present because I was in the hospital recovering from a seizure. Many of them were hoping to talk to me, since I was the one who did most of the stunts and always seemed to be drunker in the videos. I was glad to disappoint the assholes and happy to be left alone, even if it was in a hospital bed.

The media recovered quickly from their disappointment as Donnie launched into the stories behind the *Bumfights* videos. He related how he and I would meet Ryan behind the Vons shopping center and how we were given alcohol to do stunts for the camera. He described how each stunt grew more dangerous than the last one. The cameras clicked, tapes rolled, tape recorders whizzed, and pencils scratched against notepads on the courthouse steps in front of him. Donnie described, in detail, the injuries that both of us had suffered as a result of the stunts.

As he talked, the cameras covering the press conference turned toward the reporters. I squinted at the sea of faces, looking for some kind of reaction, then frowned when I saw that all they were interested in was getting every word Donnie said on film, tape, and paper. It suddenly occurred to me that these people with cameras didn't give much more of a shit about me than the last group that had pointed cameras at me. Everyone seemed to be making a buck off Donnie and me.

They cut back to Donnie as he rambled on, answering questions and telling his stories. He talked about how he was offered two hundred dollars while he was inebriated to get the BUMFIGHT tattoo on his forehead.

"They told me I was a coward if I didn't get the tattoo, and I told them I'm a vet, not a coward!" Donnie exclaimed.

"Can we see the tattoo, Donnie?" a reporter called out.

Donnie took off his ever-present trucker's cap so that his forehead, the block letters spelling B-U-M-F-I-G-H-T, and the image of the beer bottle were clearly visible.

Again cameras clicked, tapes rolled, tape recorders whizzed, and pencils scratched—but not even the smallest groan of sympathy rose from the press. I let out one of my own.

Once all the questions had been answered and Donnie had sufficiently detailed the "bums'" side of the story, Browne Greene ended the press conference. I looked up at the ceiling above my hospital bed, glad that I didn't have to be up there with them, but relieved that our story was getting all this attention. Maybe it would prevent guys like Ryan and his buddies from doing stuff like this again.

⸺

"So after the press conference was done, the publicist, Kathy, said that Barry needed to get us some clothes for the trial," Donnie told me.

Donnie sat in the corner of my hospital room and talked while I got dressed. Barry stood outside the room, talking to the doctor as Donnie filled me in on the rest of their day.

Barry had taken Donnie to the Ascot Shop in La Jolla, where his friend Bart tended the store. Donnie watched him trustingly hand his gold card over to Bart.

"You should've heard Barry, laying it on thick—how I'm a vet, about the *Bumfights*, being homeless, and the whole thing," Donnie said.

"Did he give you a free shirt?" I asked, still groggy.

"For a while there I think Barry thought his friend was going to— or at least give us a good deal. His friend treated me like royalty. It was really weird, man."

"So what happened?"

"I picked out a shirt." Donnie grinned devilishly as I sat down in a chair next to him to wait for Barry.

"So?" I said, getting slightly annoyed at the Donnie Show.

"I picked out a shirt that ran Barry $145." Donnie snickered.

I managed a chuckle.

"I thought you'd like that," Donnie said.

But the mood in the room quickly changed when the doctor followed Barry in and told me that he had major concerns about my health. The crux of it was that over a dozen years of living on the streets—nearly three times that long as an alcoholic and now the list of *Bumfights*-related injuries, including the serious head injury from Mark Oldfield that had caused my double vision—had left my state of health beyond critical. The last seizure was my body's version of a serious wake-up call that, apparently, I wasn't supposed to ignore. He advised me to follow up at the VA hospital for further testing and treatment. Besides strokes and heart attacks, I was at risk for all other kinds of cardiovascular problems as well as disorientation and hallucinations. To put it simply, I was a damn mess.

But even that warning didn't scare me enough to make me behave. A few days later I went through five hours of every test known to mankind at the VA hospital. Adding insult to injury was the long wait to talk to the doctor at the end of the marathon. I was pissed and at this point didn't really give a damn about what was causing the seizures, although I felt sure it had something to do with the sudden booze cutbacks. I had a surefire way of fixing that problem if I could find a way to make Barry just get me the hell out of there.

My first strategy was to be the nastiest, most foul-mouthed son of a bitch they'd ever seen, and maybe they'd throw me out of the hospital. Then they sent in a blonde nurse—a perfect ten in my book. She did her best to charm me into staying and being less of a pain in the ass. I backed off, but only a little. I didn't want to let Barry think that this kind of thing was all it took to control me.

The doctor finally told me that I had severe head injuries and serious injuries to my optic nerves. That probably explained the double vision, not to mention the seizures, I figured. But before they could do anything about treating my head injuries, the doctor said, I needed to get cleaned up—and fast. The VA had a rehabilitation program, and they could admit me there.

"But you need to be sober for three full days to be admitted," Barry said.

I watched Barry sink into a chair. "Screw you," I told him.

I was pissed at how everyone was making all these plans about what I should and shouldn't do, and doing so right there in front of me.

"You could be dead in eight months if you don't do the rehab, Rufus," the doctor said somberly.

"Fine, whatever," I said.

I got up and left. Barry followed a few steps behind. We walked out to the parking lot in silence. In the car Barry said, "You need to do the rehab, Rufus. You've heard what they have been telling you. In case you haven't figured it out yet, you are not exactly the healthiest guy in the world."

"Fuck you," I told him.

Now I was really pissed. I wanted to jump out of the car, roll down the road, and take my chances. Hell, the doctor had said I was gonna die anyway, so maybe this way would be easier. And to be honest I was sick of the whole boozing and withdrawal cycles. I was getting too old for this shit. All the highs and lows, the withdrawal shakes, and the running around trying to get booze money were exhausting. But I sure as hell wasn't going to go into any fucking cold-turkey detox program just because these assholes thought I should. What gave them the right?

Lost in these thoughts, I suddenly noticed that Barry had taken a detour and wasn't following the familiar route back to the E-Z 8, where Donnie awaited us.

"What are you doin'?" I grumbled.

As much as I hated the boozing cycle, I had to admit that about now I could really use a drink. My body was screaming for it, especially after the day of torture at the hospital.

Barry pulled the car into the parking lot of the Merkley Mitchell Mortuary. What in hell were we doing there?

"Someone you know die?" I asked. In truth I was terrified. All I could think about was the last time I'd set foot in a funeral home—the day we had buried my mother.

"No one's dead just yet. Come on," he snapped.

"No damn way." I folded my arms and refused to budge from the car.

I hoped that he was buying my convincing show of anger. All I could see was the image of my mother's coffin. I worked hard to keep the wall of anger up so my true feelings wouldn't show.

"Get the hell out of the car right now, Rufus," Barry said in an angry tone of voice that I had never heard before. "This is my last shot at trying to help you. I promised Browne Greene and the others that I could keep you and Donnie in check, and you're making me look like shit. Like a damned failure! Get out now, or I swear you and Donnie are both out on the streets again!"

"Fine, whatever. That's what we want anyway," I said stubbornly.

"You might want to think that over and check with Donnie first, because that also means no more food, no more cigarettes, and no more booze money that you've been hawking the cigarettes for." He practically shouted at me, causing some other people to stare. By this time I had reluctantly climbed out of the car, and we were standing nose to nose with each other, and people watching us probably thought we were going to start duking it out.

That last part at least made my eyes open wider.

"And the laundry money you've also been spending on liquor. Yeah, that's right. I'm on to your little game, and that's it. I'm done. Either come with me right now, or start walking back to La Mesa or wherever the hell it is you want to die."

Once again I pictured my mother's coffin. No, I wasn't doing this for Barry. It was for Lucille, in her memory.

A moment later I sucked in a breath and followed him into the building. After a brief conversation with the funeral director, Barry led me into a room full of caskets for sale.

"Here's the deal, Rufus. You either check into the rehab program immediately, or I buy you a casket."

"Screw—"

He interrupted me. "Because we both know that without the program, you'll be dead in a year anyway."

I decided to shut the hell up just long enough to think about this for a moment.

Barry pressed on. "So what's it going to be? The casket and back to the street with Donnie to die, or twenty-eight days that will save your life and hopefully change it for the better? Come on, my friend. I'm sparing no expense on your coffin."

"Don't I get to think about it?" I snapped.

Barry whipped out his wallet and the gold card again and shoved a finger in my face. "No, you don't. I'm sick of this shit, and I've had enough of you guys jerking me around. I'm ready to buy you a casket right now and leave you here if you don't swear—swear on the lives of your children and on your mother's grave, Rufus—that you will do the rehab program."

That was a low blow. I was exhausted, the room was starting to go hazy, and now on top of that my heart was starting to hurt. I thought I was about to have another seizure, and I grabbed for the closest thing I could find to steady myself—the handle of a coffin. It was bad enough that my kids were telling everyone that their father was dead. Making it the truth seemed like the worst thing possible to do to them.

"Yeah, okay. I'll do it," I finally said, my eyes cast downward.

Barry nodded and put a hand on my shoulder. "Thank God," he sighed.

As we left the funeral parlor, a family with young children was entering. I kept my eyes down so Barry wouldn't see me starting to tear up. If I was ever going to do this, it was now or never.

CHAPTER 13

RECOVERY

"I don't like friggin' hamburgers," I told Barry angrily. Just because I had agreed to get sober didn't mean my attitude toward Barry was about to change.

The day after the unexpected mortuary visit, when he arrived at the E-Z 8 with lunch, I was uncharacteristically alone in the room. Barry handed me a bag of In-N-Out hamburgers.

"What do you mean you don't like hamburgers?" he asked.

"Every day it's nothing but hamburgers. You're in the door, out the door without a word. Barry, you're just like the label on that bag, in and out. You...never talk to me!"

Those were more words than I had ever said to the guy. Prior to that the most I had felt like saying to him was to tell him to go fuck himself. Today I felt the need to expand on that, just so he wouldn't think I was stupid or something.

"Okay, what else?" he asked.

I curled up on the bed and dug into my lunch. I didn't say anything for a couple of minutes. I just ate and occasionally glanced at Barry as he sat at a table near the door. It was strange without Donnie there to monopolize the conversation and "kiss Barry's ass," as he always called it. I finished my lunch and threw away the trash. He continued to stare at me.

"Did I ever tell you why I hired you and Donnie?" he finally asked.

"I already know. Mr. Hawkins threatened you with Jesus," I said.

"You think that's why I hired you? Because of Jesus? For God's sake, Rufus, I'm a *Jew*!" He laughed.

"Why, then?"

"Because I was positive that you guys wouldn't show up, and I knew if I just said yes, Old Mr. Hawkins would shut up and leave me alone."

"You're kidding. Really?" I said in surprise.

"Yes. But over time my feelings about you and Donnie changed. I didn't see you as drunken bums anymore, just a couple of guys who happened to work for me. Another thing about being Jewish is that I'm mechanically challenged." He grinned. "So I was impressed by your skills and your attention to detail. Anyway, it's interesting that you think it was some kind of divine intervention."

"I don't believe in no divine intervention."

"That's surprising to me, Rufus. Because it seems to me the fact that you're even sitting here alive is a miracle," he said.

I shrugged. "Jesus has never done nothin' for me. If he was ever with me, he left a long time ago, and I haven't seen any sign of him since."

"It breaks my heart to hear you say that," Barry said, much to my surprise again.

"Why the hell—"

"Not because of the Jesus part specifically…I'm just wondering where you get your strength from."

"I don't want to die," I said. "I decided that in Las Vegas. You really didn't have to bring me to the funeral home…but it sure was a nice touch."

"How so?"

"It made me realize why I don't want to die. I wanna live to see my kids again."

From then on I felt safe enough to open up even more. I talked about my family, about Swainsboro, how I actually was worried about my drinking, and more.

By the end of the day I felt like I really could trust Barry. As he prepared to leave, I pointed at his weathered, worn, and ever-present baseball cap, with the distinctive *B* embroidered on the front. There was something I'd been meaning to ask him for the longest time.

"What's that *B* stand for anyway?"

"The Boston Red Sox. My favorite baseball team," he said.

"Oh." I was disappointed.

"What's the matter?"

"I thought it stood for *bum*," I said.

He laughed. "You know, Rufus, you and Donnie are just like my Red Sox."

"Why's that?"

"You're always breaking my heart," he told me. This was, of course, prior to 2004, when his team stopped breaking hearts and became world champions.

"You know, I really do want to get better," I said.

"Good. I'm going to do everything in my power to help you, Rufus—with or without divine intervention."

I muttered something that I suppose was a thank-you as Barry walked out the door.

—·—

The next day the countdown clock started for me. Barry managed
to get Donnie on board to keep me sober for the three days required
prior to admission. But this didn't necessarily mean that Donnie
stopped going out and drinking on his own.

By the third day of the agonizing withdrawal at the E-Z 8, I was
a mess. I paced the room like a caged animal, occasionally trying to
push Donnie away from the door so I could get out on the streets
and find some relief. I couldn't sleep at all, and my mind raced with
thoughts of what life would be like without alcohol. I battled the
demon in my head, the one that would tell me, *Just one more drink.
Just one more little drink, Rufus.* Those same demons were quick to
remind me that I was a real failure.

During one of the times I was crashed out on the bed, sweating
and shaking, I heard Donnie on the phone with Barry. Donnie's voice
seemed to be coming down a tin tunnel from miles away.

"Barry, you've gotta come help me. I don't know how much longer
I can control him," Donnie said.

I passed out briefly, and when I woke up I couldn't move my
arms and legs. My mind panicked, but my body still wouldn't move.
I managed to lift my head just enough to see that I was tied to the
bed with sheets, wrapped up as tightly as a mummy. I decided then
that I was too damned exhausted to fight back. I looked at Donnie,
who was smoking a cigarette at the foot of the bed and purposely
averting his eyes. Barry stood outside the room, talking on his cell
phone as usual. *This stupid program had better be worth all the
bullshit,* I thought.

—·—

The next morning—October 29, 2002—Barry drove me to the VA hospital. "Are you nervous?" he asked as we strode along the covered walkway toward the entrance.

"Just a little jittery," I said, trying to control my withdrawal tremors.

"That's not what I meant. Are you nervous in general?"

"I'm losing my best friend and lover of nearly forty years. What do you think?" I asked as we neared the admissions area.

"The bottle, you mean," he said.

"Yeah. It's like every step I'm taking down this hall with you, I'm reliving every moment of that relationship—good and bad."

He looked at me and nodded. We entered the admissions area, and my entrance into the recovery program began. Once I passed the blood and urine tests, I was officially on the road to recovery.

The VA program was rigid. The first seven days equated to a total lockdown: nobody leaves the facility for any reason. During this time I went through the worst stages of alcohol withdrawal. I barely ate. I couldn't sleep at night. And I sweated buckets, soaking my hospital sheets from lights-out till dawn. My body was rebelling against my mind, and my mind was trying to force its way out of my body.

In the middle of one of those early torturous nights I tossed and turned in my bed, fighting off the worst night sweats, tremors, and body aches that I have ever felt. I was so out of my frigging mind that I couldn't tell what was real, what was a hallucination, and what was a dream. It all seemed to blur together like a kaleidoscope, swirling seamlessly from one scene to the next. One of the other guys in detox had to be put in restraints when he thought that creatures from outer space were going to beam him up to their spaceship.

While I was never put in restraints, there was one time when the kaleidoscope turned and a new scene materialized at the foot of my bed. This one was real enough to give me the strength to prop myself up in bed on my elbows.

"Oh my God!" I gasped.

My daughter Stephanie stood in front of me. She was a little girl, but I couldn't tell how old she was. That part didn't matter so much, because even in my delusional state I knew she wasn't real.

She smiled at me and held out her hand. As I reached out my fingertips, Stephanie's face started to change. My eyes filled with tears. Even though the sight of her was just a figment of my imagination, I didn't want to lose my little girl again.

The image of my daughter now transformed into Jesus Christ himself. I sat propped up on my elbows, mouth open wide.

My child, if you want to know me, look into the faces of your children, Jesus said.

I collapsed back onto the bed, exhausted. It was the last thing I remembered that night.

While the first seven days of the program were a physical challenge, after that it was mostly psychological. I struggled with the challenge of giving up my best friend of four decades. Actually alcohol was more of a lover to me. Especially since it had managed to jealously push away every woman I had been close to in my life. This was a raging battle I fought every moment of every day in the program— and afterward too. For forty years I had slept with this mistress. She made me forget everything else. Now I was fighting the greatest battle of my life so far to free myself from her once and for all.

———

One day the psychologist leading my group asked each resident to think about why he drank. It sounded like such a simple question:

"Why do you drink?" I remembered asking this very question when I was fourteen.

It had been a sticky August evening when I had first posed that question. I enjoyed the cool metal chair I sat on behind the convenience store while playing cards with the old locals. I looked around in amazement at all the empty liquor and beer bottles lined up on the concrete. It seemed like we'd only been playing cards for a little while, but there were more bottles out there than inside the store. I had been working up the nerve to ask this question for weeks now, and I felt like I couldn't hold off anymore.

"Why do you guys drink?" I finally blurted out. Then I pushed my chair back from the table, ready to run, because I didn't know how they'd respond.

To my surprise the men burst out in raucous laughter. But they also avoided eye contact with one another and me. Finally they spoke, and each man gave a different reason.

"It helps us to enjoy each other's company more."

"It helps me to relax."

"I don't know. Just kinda goes with the cards and the evening and all."

The way in which each man offered his reason made it clear to me that they didn't want to be asked about this anymore.

Back then, as a teenager, I remembered being relieved that it was apparently no big deal to drink. It was perfectly acceptable. Now I look back at those old men and realize the struggles that some of them were probably going through. I saw how they had made getting together and drinking every night such a big part of their lives. Back then I'd looked up to them for this. Now I feel sorry for them.

———

Each day the VA program started with an exercise class at seven in the morning. The class wasn't exactly high-impact aerobics. The instructors let each person exercise as much or as little as he or she wanted. This resulted in some people merely standing and waving their arms in the air during jumping jacks and lying on the floor during push-ups and sit-ups. Because I was suffering the effects of alcohol withdrawal and sleep deprivation, I wasn't the most energetic member of the class, but I tried to keep up with some of the more active ones. After that came a brief break and then breakfast. Overall the daily regimen was a busy one to keep the residents active and our minds occupied. There were Alcoholics Anonymous meetings, lots of group therapy, and even a safe-sex class. (I wondered who were we supposed to have sex with when every moment of every day was scheduled?)

One of my favorite things to do was work in the hospital hobby shop. The other residents and I would sculpt with clay, paint pictures, and construct model cars. I would usually visit the shop twice a week to work on the latter.

The program residents were divided into pods—two separate groups with officers, chore lists, etc. This was also how they were divided up for their group meetings.

Barry visited me every day, bringing supplies and cigarettes. On day number seven, when my head finally felt like it was clearing up a little, I had a special request for him.

"Barry, I really want to spend my time here doing something important—something that will help me once I get out. I want to learn something."

"Want me to bring you some books to read?" he asked.

"Yeah, that'd be great…but my eyesight's all messed up, so I don't know if I'd even be able to read them."

"We could try books on tape. What kinds of books do you want?"

I thought for a moment. "Not so much books. I wanna learn more words, make my vocabulary better. I'm sure that would help me with finding jobs in the future."

Barry told me how excited he was that I wanted to become more educated. The next day he plunked a huge book onto the table in the recreation room.

"What's that?" I asked.

"A large-print dictionary."

"Wow."

Barry smiled. "You're welcome."

Once I had become well acquainted with the dictionary, Barry started bringing me other books, including one of his personal favorites, a large-print version of the popular *Tuesdays with Morrie*. He loved that book, and he said that he'd even met the author, Mitch Albom.

One day I requested another book. "I was wondering if you could bring me a Bible."

"What brought this on?" Barry asked in surprise.

"I think I had one of those divine-intervention things you mentioned before."

"Sure. You got it."

———

The VA program was well structured, with so many required activities that there was never a dull moment. But the required activities I hated the most were the "talk about your feelings" classes and weekly groups.

The staff members running the classes and groups were mostly shrinks, social workers, and nurses from nearby University of California, San Diego (UCSD). They would try to get me to talk about myself, what I had been feeling, and the emotions behind those feelings.

I didn't even know what feelings like "happy" meant, so I didn't know what the hell I was supposed to be saying when they asked these weird questions. I'd be sitting there, feeling lost and pissed off, having just given up my best friend of numerous years, and these people wanted to know all kinds of stuff about my feelings. By the end of these classes I was about ready to explode. I would usually head outside to the hospital grounds to smoke a cigarette and blow off some steam.

One day while attending one of the feelings groups, I felt like crap. I'd had little sleep, I had the jitters, and everyone in the group was talking simultaneously—even though the rule was one person at a time. Suddenly, in the midst of the spinning chaos, one of the most caring people I'd met there looked over at me. She was a psychologist and a professor from UCSD. She would always come over and hold your hand and listen to you intently as you talked. And when you were done, she would ask respectfully, "Is it okay if we ask the group for feedback?" I usually felt comfortable and at peace around her. But as soon she looked at me on this day, I knew what she wanted, and I got nervous.

"Rufus, I know you've got something to say," she said, cutting through the chaos.

"Nah, I haven't got anything to say," I responded.

"Come on, Rufus. I can tell you have something to say," the sweet woman persisted.

I sighed. She wasn't going to let me off the hook, and I knew it. So I decided to get this over with.

"You're goddamned right I got something to say," I said loudly. All eyes in the group were now on me. The room fell silent.

"To begin with, I don't want to be here in this stupid place. I'm tired of it! Every time I want some rest, I gotta go somewhere else!"

"How do you feel about that?" another staff member asked.

"I'm pissed off, and I gotta get some rest! I just gotta go somewhere," I continued.

At that point a nurse took me aside and found that my blood pressure had skyrocketed. Their concern set off a bunch of panic. My favorite psychologist helped to calm me down. She told me not to worry about the feelings exercise or the group homework and to just take my time. I was grateful to both of them because I wasn't sure what else I would have said or done if they had made me stay in that group any longer.

Now free to blow off some steam, I put my sunglasses on. But instead of going outside, I wandered around the hospital. There was a rule that you couldn't wear sunglasses in group meetings, but there was nothing in the rules about wandering around the hospital and wearing them, so I figured I was okay. I shuffled aimlessly down the hallways, happy to be lost in my thoughts—or more specifically, not having to think about a damned thing for the time being.

As I started to feel better, I heard the call overhead for my next meeting. When I made it back to my floor, the program director, Brian, confronted me.

"Hey! Take those sunglasses off," he exclaimed.

My previous calm immediately disappeared and turned into a fresh round of rage, now directed at this guy.

"For your information I was just getting ready to take them off and go into the damned meeting!" I bellowed.

"I need to talk to you, Rufus," Brian said, ushering me into his office.

I sat in the chair across from Brian's desk with my arms folded, like a pouting child sent to the principal's office for some indiscretion. I was determined not to give the guy an inch.

"Rufus, you can't walk around here with your sunglasses on like you're always doing," Brian began.

The lecture continued, but I didn't much care what else Brian had to say. I really wanted to give this guy a piece of my mind, but I knew that once I started, I would most likely go overboard and probably get kicked out of the program. So I thought about it as Brian continued going over every little thing that I had ever done wrong. I thought this was extremely unfair, not to mention humiliating. I also thought back to the way I handled confrontations all my life, like with the high school principal. Reacting so impulsively back then was the reason why I quit school. If I was supposed to be changing, then I couldn't let stuff like this get to me anymore. Still, it wasn't easy to listen to this.

When Brian was done, I stormed out of his office and into the recovery room. I was still thinking about whether to turn around and confront Brian. And then I ran right into Barry.

Barry laughed. "Rufus, what's the matter? There's steam coming out of your ears!"

"Fuc—" I stopped myself quickly. Old habits really did die hard.

"What is it?" he asked.

I told him everything that had happened. "He won't get away with this shit!" I finished.

"Rufus, you have to go and apologize to him," Barry said.

"What the hell!" I exploded again. I couldn't believe he wanted me to apologize.

"Rufus, trust me. You need to apologize. This is all part of the program. It's a process," Barry explained.

Some other residents looked at us briefly, but then they returned to whatever they were doing. They'd seen worse in this program, where one of the main objectives was to push the addict's buttons to teach him how to deal with outside pressures. A nurse soon joined us, and she supported what Barry was telling me.

"We need to see how you react under stress," she added. "It's a lot worse when you get back into the real world."

After a couple more minutes of convincing I finally apologized to Brian. At that moment apologizing felt like I was admitting that I had done something wrong. In hindsight I realized that this was a turning point for me: being able to deal with anger without drinking, retreating into my shell, cussing the other person out, or doing all three.

Once I apologized, Brian's attitude toward me seemed to change. He was extremely respectful to me from then on, adopting an "it's all behind us" attitude. Brian told me that if I had any problems or needed to speak with him about anything, his door was always open. I continued on with the program, and it went so much better after that.

—·—

When graduation day from the twenty-eight-day program finally arrived, Barry asked me what I would like as a graduation gift. We'd been off the hospital grounds for lunch and were driving back when he sprang the question.

I thought about it for a bit. "Two things, actually," I said.

"Really." Barry laughed at my boldness.

"It's not what you're thinking. One of them is that I want a gift to give to this woman psychologist. I really enjoyed her class."

"That's sweet, Rufus. Sure, let's do that."

I smiled and felt encouraged enough to make my other request. "The second thing, and I know it's a lot…"

"Go ahead," Barry encouraged me.

"I would like a suit. I've never owned one before. I could wear it to job interviews and in court for all that legal stuff. Besides, the counselors here told me that it's important to look good because it makes you feel good about yourself."

He immediately drove to a local Men's Wearhouse and helped me pick out a suit, tie, dress shirt, socks, and shoes. All dressed up, I looked at my reflection in the dressing-room mirror.

"Rufus, you look better than I do!" he exclaimed happily.

"It wouldn't be hard. All you ever wear is a baseball cap, sweatshirt, and jeans. Now who's the bum?" I joked.

"Hey, I thought we were friends now."

I knew that last part was meant in good fun. This was a nice turn of events.

"Yeah, Barry, we are friends," I said.

"And you're like a whole new person," Barry added. "I have the feeling that you're going to be able to accomplish whatever you want in life from this point on, Rufus." That made me smile.

Next Barry helped me pick out an expensive bottle of perfume for the psychologist. When I got back to the recovery unit later that day and gave the counselor her gift, I saw her get teary-eyed. I usually look away when people show emotion. This time I didn't.

But while I was making remarkable strides in my recovery, one person still weighed on my mind: my best friend back at the E-Z 8.

That same day I asked Barry, "What's happening with Donnie?"

He sighed.

"That bad?"

"He hates being alone, but I'm trying to keep him from going out on the street. I'm afraid we'd never see him again."

"You're right. We probably wouldn't," I said.

"So do you think he'd do well in this program?" he asked.

I pondered that for a minute, trying to figure out how to tell Barry about the Donnie I knew versus the one who always put on the charming front for him.

"I'm not sure. Donnie doesn't like being told what to do," I finally said.

He scowled. "Are you kidding me? And you do?"

"Donnie's actually worse when you cross him, though. He…gets really out of control," I said cautiously.

"So you're saying it probably won't work."

I shrugged. "I don't know. Give it a try if you want. Ask him about it. He at least deserves a shot."

The truth, as I suspected, was that while I worked hard on my road to recovery, Donnie continued to play host to the entire homeless population of La Mesa back at the E-Z 8. And on top of that Charming Donnie had become Pain in the Ass Donnie.

Unfortunately, while I was succeeding in my recovery at the VA, Donnie was doing the exact opposite. He drank more, trashed the motel room more, smoked more, and essentially had become more of a pain in the ass for Barry. So when Barry decided to take my advice and try to get Donnie to enter the VA program, I knew it was a long shot.

Donnie, however, surprised everyone and agreed. And for the first three weeks, he coasted through the program without a complaint or a problem. He even became president of his pod on day number twenty. True to his promise Donnie had become a model resident in the recovery program, and Barry and I could not have been more proud.

Delighted by his progress, Barry arranged to reward Donnie on the following Saturday, just four days before his graduation, with a trip to the Aerospace Museum at Balboa Park.

But when Barry arrived as promised outside the VA hospital at 9 a.m. to pick him up, Donnie wasn't there. Barry looked everywhere around the hospital but could not find him. Finally he checked with the rehab office to find out what was going on. After some persuasion he got the truth from a woman at the front desk.

"This resident broke the rules. He went down the street to the 7-Eleven, purchased some alcohol, and drank it on the hospital grounds. He had to leave the program," she said.

"Do you know where he is?" Barry asked, panicked.

"Sorry, sir, I don't. But in our experience most residents who fail to complete the program go back to wherever they were prior to coming here."

Barry had officially checked Donnie out of the E-Z 8 weeks ago, when Donnie moved to the VA hospital. So he knew in his heart exactly what that meant. Donnie was back on the streets of La Mesa, right where it had all started.

When Barry broke the news to me soon after, I wasn't surprised. "Well, that's the Donnie I know," I said.

"Really? You predicted this?" he asked.

"I didn't predict it, but I'm not surprised at it either. Donnie says whatever he needs to say to get what he wants. He also likes to show off. I think he probably just did this to make you proud."

"So what do you think happened?"

I shrugged. "They're really tough on you in there. They break you down—kinda like boot camp all over again."

"But Donnie made it through boot camp—"

"That was the pre-Vietnam, pre-homeless, pre-alcoholic Donnie. These days he loses it if people try and boss him around. With *Bumfights*, I think he felt like he was using Ryan and those guys because he was getting booze. But once in a while he fought back when he thought they were pushing him too far."

"I just thought…" Barry said. "I mean, he's so personable. I just would've predicted…" He still couldn't wrap his mind around this unlikely outcome.

"You thought that *he* would get sober and *I'd* stay a drunk." I finished his thought.

"Exactly. So what happened?" he asked.

"I *wanted* to get sober. I wasn't willing to live my life like that anymore, and like you said, I was going to die if I did. I wanted it, and Donnie doesn't."

"I know that now. The more determined you became to get yourself straight, the more I started to see how genuine you were, and also that Donnie, despite his outgoing personality, was a good salesman. Like you said, he didn't want the same thing you did."

What I didn't say was that I had another reason for wanting the recovery so bad. As one of my assignments in the program I had—with help from my sister, Jenny—gotten in touch with my daughter Stephanie in an attempt to make things right again. Or at least convince her that she really did have a living father who would do everything in his power to stop causing her such pain and embarrassment. As it turned out, that would be easier said than done.

When I finally received a letter from Stephanie, she informed me how she, and also my nephew, knew exactly what I had been up to. Surfing the Web one night, they had inadvertently come upon an online *Bumfights* clip. Somehow she had heard that I was involved in these videos, but she didn't know the whole truth. Now she watched in horror as her father got drunk out of his mind, lay belly down on a skateboard, and careened down a concrete ravine toward a gigantic concrete column and some railroad tracks. They were horrified. My daughter made it quite clear to me that watching the video was one of the lowest, most humiliating points of her life.

"I can't believe you would ever live like that," she'd written.

After I read the letter in which Stephanie described what my actions had put her and my nephew through that night, as they stared in horror at their computer screen, I knew that I had no choice but to complete the rehab program. I vowed never to put my friends and loved ones through anything like that ever again. I was so angry at myself, angry at Ryan McPherson and his pals, and disgusted by the fact that I could've sunk so low in my life. I felt like I was in hell.

———

The next step in my treatment would take place at an intermediate recovery facility. While I was still at the VA hospital, I had to fill out applications for other programs I would be interested in after graduation. I chose the Vietnam Veterans of San Diego (VVSD), now called the Veterans Village of San Diego. After that it was a matter of their choosing me.

This included getting in touch with the center's director, Rick Hastings, every week and visiting him on Saturdays. Rick was six feet three inches of all muscle with a deep, resonating voice—even more intimidating in person. He was like an army drill sergeant. I felt instantly intimidated.

"This program is like boot camp. You've been there before, so you know what that's like," Hastings barked at me from across his desk.

"Yes, sir," I said.

During my final week in the VA program, as instructed, I phoned Rick one last time to tell him how much I wanted to go to the VVSD. Rick told me to come to his office at lunchtime, and I didn't dare refuse.

"You have to change everything—and I mean everything. If you screw up, there's no second chance," Hastings said.

"Yes, sir."

I was admitted to the VVSD late in 2002. Rick Hastings had already laid out most of the rules for me before I even checked in. I would live there, at the compound, as the residents called it, for eleven months—nearly all of 2003. For the first month residents were not allowed to go *anywhere* except to doctor's appointments. Even then they had to go with a chaperone and show their counselor proof of the appointment ahead of time.

The VVSD was a welcome change after nearly a month in the sterile atmosphere of the VA hospital. This place was like a village, with two parallel rows of one-bedroom cottages, complete with front porches for people watching. A dirt path down the center led to a dining hall, laundry room, recreation room, and other common areas.

The daily routine at the VVSD began much like the one at the VA. Chow came at six in the morning, and the first class followed at seven. Fortunately there weren't so many feelings classes this time around.

These classes focused more on concrete skill sets and the trouble spots that could cause a relapse rather than abstract emotions.

The classes were different in another way—some might call them brutal. Suddenly the nice nurses, caring counselors, and guys like Brian making me say what I was thinking seemed like a walk in the park. The VVSD classes were feedback groups, where every member was encouraged to share whatever he thought about what the last guy said, openly and honestly.

A typical exchange in the group might start with, "What do you think of Joe?" Another group member would respond, "I think he's a jerk and a piece of shit."

I watched a few members almost get into fistfights as a result, but I always managed to stay out of trouble. I was thankful to the people who had prepared me to handle situations like this.

Each day would be capped off with dinner, followed by an AA meeting. I also volunteered to be secretary at the AA meetings. As secretary I had to manage the money allocated for coffee supplies and other necessities. This was the first time in a long while that I was responsible for anything related to anyone outside of myself.

This rekindled a familiar feeling: I remembered how much I enjoyed working. After my first thirty days at the VVSD, I called Barry and asked if I could go back to work for him during the day. He agreed, and for a while I added that to my daily routines, always returning in time to perform my duties as secretary at the nightly AA meetings.

Next on my agenda was a job repairing wheelchairs for the Wellness and Vocational Enrichment Clinic (WAVE Program). Getting this job wasn't easy. I had to meet first with a psychiatrist from the program to gain approval. *No big deal,* I thought. I'd been meeting with shrinks and counselors for a couple of months now. This particular doctor, however, was a challenge from the start.

I showed up for my appointment dressed in my usual blue jeans, T-shirt, and tennis shoes. Strike one, I soon found out. Apparently I was supposed to dress in slacks and nice shoes. The conversation only went downhill from there.

"What are your problems, Rufus?" the doctor asked.

I started listing my physical problems: the *Bumfights*-related injuries, double vision, the head injury, and more. But the doctor shook his head impatiently and interrupted.

"Why aren't you telling me about your problems with alcohol?" he asked.

"What the hell are you asking me that for?" I said angrily. "You've got that computer right in front of you with all that information."

"I want to hear about it from you. Tell me why you think you've had all these problems and how you feel about that."

"This meeting's over. The hell with you—I'm outta here!"

I stormed out of the doctor's office and returned to the VVSD. Marching into the office of my counselor, Jim Mooney, I told him what had happened.

"Jim, I really wanna work at WAVE, but I just can't deal with that guy again," I said.

"Let me talk to him. I'll see what I can do," Jim reassured me.

Jim made the call and persuaded me to go back to see the WAVE psychiatrist a second time. This visit began well, but soon he was starting in on me again. He told me that I needed to get a haircut, groom myself, get rid of the tattoos, and dress better.

"Fuck this. I'm outta here!" I exclaimed, storming out a second time.

And once again I went to see Jim.

"Here I am trying to get into this program and get me a better job, and this guy is treating me like shit! I can't deal with him, Jim. There's gotta be another way."

I was completely frustrated. Here I was finally trying to do the right thing and turn my life around. But people were getting in the way, saying that it wasn't worth taking a chance on me.

Jim calmed me down and called the psychiatrist again, trying to smooth things over. If only I could make it through just one meeting with this guy, I could get the job repairing wheelchairs and move forward with my life.

For the next meeting an impartial third party, a woman doctor, sat in. The whole atmosphere in the room changed instantly. I realized this the minute she walked in. I really wanted to get into this program, and I knew that this would be my last shot. Thankfully, the final meeting went smoothly, and the psychiatrist approved me for the WAVE Program.

Remembering the valuable lessons I had learned about the power of an apology, I paused at the door on the way out. I looked the psychiatrist in the eye.

"I know you really do have my best interests in mind. I think you really want to help me, and I appreciate that. Thank you," I said.

We shook hands.

"I think everything's going to be okay, Rufus," the other doctor said.

She proved to be a sage. I got along well with my fellow residents at the VVSD, enjoyed my role as secretary at the AA meetings, and now had the prospect of steady work. I was even getting along well with the compound's drill instructor, Rick Hastings. But that didn't mean Rick was going to lengthen the short leash he had on me or any of the other residents.

We residents understood one thing: when Rick Hastings told you there were no second chances, he meant it. I had heard horror stories from the other residents about the wrath of Rick, which was unleashed when a resident was caught intoxicated—or even if he just assumed they were. They didn't just get kicked out of the program; they got their asses handed to them as Rick bodily removed them from the property. So I knew from the outset not to mess around there.

Besides, my recovery was going really well. I felt like a new man these days. Sure I regretted the absence of my mistress every once in a while, especially when things got hard. But for the most part my health improved greatly, and my head cleared up so I could think straight. I had no desire to go back to my old life.

Unfortunately Rick Hastings had seen and heard this song and dance before. His residents' actions were the only things that spoke to him. Words were empty promises.

One afternoon Barry returned me to the VVSD after I'd had the majority of my teeth removed by an oral surgeon. Jim, whom I came to respect and trust a lot, had recommended the treatment. My unhealthy lifestyle had contributed to periodontal disease, my gums were a mess, and I was almost always in pain.

That day Barry half dragged, half carried me along, as I could barely stand. I also appeared inebriated from the Novocain I'd been given.

We'd almost made it to the front porch of my cottage, when Hastings spotted us. "Are you kidding me?" he bellowed, storming over to confront me.

Barry tried to explain, but Hastings cut him off. "How dare you show up at my facility drunk? You lying son of a bitch, how dare you drink while on my watch?" he yelled.

"Rick, Rufus is not drunk." Barry finally managed to get a word in.

"What do you mean he's not drunk? Look at him!" Hastings jabbed his finger at me as I hung over Barry's shoulder like a rag doll.

"Rufus had major dental surgery today," Barry said.

Hastings looked me up and down and even sniffed my breath before finally accepting the fact. He then relieved Barry of my dead-weight, carried me through the front door of my cottage, and plopped me down on the bed.

Suddenly the weight of the past few grueling months in recovery, combined with forty years as an alcoholic and twelve years homeless, came crashing down on me. I felt like I had been awake for a thousand years. I wanted to become a responsible member of society and to earn some respect. I wanted to build a healthy relationship with my family. No longer did I want people to think of me only as a snarling, drunken bum.

Still, this was too much for my head. Rolling over, I fell asleep.

CHAPTER 14
COURTS *and* CAMERAS

WHILE I CONTINUED WITH MY RECOVERY, THE CRIMINAL court case against the *Bumfights* filmmakers, and the damned media circus, continued at the El Cajon courthouse.

The defendants in the case were Ryan McPherson, Zachary Bubeck, Daniel Tanner, and Michael Slyman. There was a lot of legal talk and technicalities going on throughout the trial. To me, though, the main point of the criminal case was that Ryan and the filmmakers had taken advantage of the fact that Donnie and I were homeless and alcoholic, we were both injured because of it, and now they needed to be punished.

Even though Donnie and I hadn't done anything wrong and were the victims, I was nervous throughout the entire trial. All I could think about was how much I wanted those punks to be found guilty. I wanted them to serve jail time so they could sit and think about what they'd done. I couldn't imagine how I'd feel if they were set free.

The mood across the aisle at the defense table was the opposite of our nervousness and humiliation as the details of the stunts and our drunkenness were described to the full courtroom, including television cameras. Ryan McPherson continually made faces, snickered, muttered snide remarks under his breath, and laughed. Daniel Tanner kept shooting us dirty looks. Bubeck and Slyman just looked stumped. They clearly had no idea what the hell was going on or how they'd wound up there. I wondered how many people Ryan had fooled throughout the whole mess.

Shortly after the trial and all its publicity began, word got out on the streets about those two homeless guys who were taking on some rich kids in court. Several ex-convicts told me, "I wish I could be in jail when those punks are brought in. They wouldn't be laughing then!"

Unfortunately the overwhelming video evidence of what Ryan and the others had put Donnie and me through during the past couple of years wasn't enough to seal the case against the filmmakers. The prosecution took a major hit early on, as far as believability, courtesy of one of our own witnesses: Steve Boyd, the crazy dog owner from the E-Z 8 Motel. Boyd had testified on our behalf in the trial against Mark Oldfield, the guy who'd beaten up Donnie and me, and he'd done a decent job, which was why the prosecutor was okay with using him here.

What he didn't know was that Boyd had fabricated most of the information he had given to Ryan McPherson's arresting officer, Lt. Dan Willis. The decision by Deputy DA Curtis Ross to put this nut job on the stand was the biggest mistake of the criminal trial. When Boyd took the stand this time, it became a train wreck too painful to watch. Boyd swore under oath how he himself had planned to buy the rights to the *Bumfights* series with money from his rich uncle. And that was only the beginning. My heart sank. If this was how our lawyers planned to beat McPherson and his expensive lawyers, with secret weapons like freaking Steve Boyd, Donnie and I were screwed.

Ryan's lawyers made a fool out of Boyd and the prosecution. The judge threw out Boyd's entire testimony for massive inconsistencies and for lying to the court.

Unfortunately the least valuable witnesses in the criminal trial were the victims: Donnie and me. There were, of course, credibility issues associated with two guys who were homeless alcoholics at the time of the filmings. At best we came off as unsympathetic victims.

On top of that a bunch of times during the pretrial meetings, and even in court, Donnie's and my testimonies contradicted each other. There were several periods of time that we simply could not remember, and others that we recalled one way the first time we were asked about it and a different way the second time. I tried my best to recall everything that they wanted to know. But I had been shit-faced drunk during most of the time when the stunts were filmed. And lots of people asked the same things in lots of different ways. This confused and exhausted me.

The other main problem was that, because of the fact that we were drunk or doing the stunts for even more booze, it was difficult for our lawyers to prove that we were not performing any of the stunts willingly. But in one real touching moment Donnie broke down and cried while recounting his humiliating, painful birthday night in Las Vegas with the hookers and the riding crop. While Donnie told the story, Ryan and his cronies rolled their eyes and attempted to stifle their laughter. I hated the bastards even more than I wanted to admit.

Curtis Ross argued strongly that all the defendants should do jail time. Nevertheless the combination of credibility issues, inconsistent testimonies, and a top-notch defense team were huge headaches for the prosecution. With all the video evidence before the court, the deputy district attorney had believed it would be easy to prove that the filmmakers had knowingly taken advantage of and caused a great deal of harm to two innocent homeless men. But the trial had turned into a messy game of one group's word against another's.

All the felony and misdemeanor charges were eventually dismissed for lack of evidence. The only charges left were the conspiracy ones. The four defendants pleaded guilty to those and were convicted on all counts. Their sentence was 280 hours of community service at—would you believe it—a homeless shelter! The judge warned the defendants that if they failed to complete their community service or violated any other conditions of their probation, he wouldn't hesitate to throw them in jail. Unfortunately even the judge handing down their sentence didn't silence the snickering and other disrespectful antics at the defendants' table.

Needless to say, I was angry about the sentence that the judge had handed down, and so was Barry. All the defendants' attorneys had asked for leniency, claiming that they were all so sorry, that they were young, that it was their first offense. It was all crap. But that's how the decision turned out, and we had to move on.

—

With the criminal trial over, the civil trial proceeded. This time the defendants in the case were Ray Leticia and Ty Beeson (the Vegas producers who purchased the rights to the *Bumfights* videos from Ryan McPherson for $1.5 million), Daniel Tanner, Michael Slyman, Ryan McPherson (and his father, James, since Ryan was still a minor), Zachary Bubeck, their film company, Indecline Productions, and Inkers Tattoo and Body Piercing (where Donnie got the lead BUMFIGHT tattoo on his forehead). The official charges included "emotional distress," "subjecting plaintiffs to cruel and unjust hardship in conscious disregard of their rights, maliciously intended to cause injury to plaintiffs," "causing plaintiffs to suffer anxiety, mental anguish, severe emotional and physical distress…" The list went on and on.

Our civil litigation attorneys, Browne Greene and Mark Quigley, had learned from their observations of good versus bad witnesses in the criminal case. But the major issue wasn't about witnesses; it was about whether it would be worth going forward with the trial.

The goal was to win a large judgment, including punitive damages awarded to Donnie and me for our pain and suffering. Most likely tipped off about this by their attorneys, Ryan McPherson and the other defendants immediately swore that if we won, they would each declare bankruptcy. Thus we would never see a dime of their money—specifically the proceeds from the *Bumfights* sales, which were estimated to be in the millions of dollars.

Greene and Quigley wanted to accept the sure monies from a settlement rather than risk a trial, during which they might find out that the case was not strong enough to be awarded general and punitive damages. Although a punitive award would not be erased by bankruptcy, it could possibly take years to collect, if we were even able to collect anything at all.

Apparently, every dime paid for a civil settlement would come from a homeowner's insurance policy held by Ryan McPherson's parents, since Ryan had been a minor and living with his folks at the time of the filmings. In order to receive money from the insurance company, all Greene and Quigley would have to show was that the filmmakers were simply negligent and had never intended to inflict any pain or injuries on Donnie or me. (I wondered what they *intended* to have happen by sending me down a concrete hill on a skateboard.)

In order to be awarded punitive damages, Greene and Quigley

would have to prove to a jury that the actions by McPherson and company were intentional and specifically done to cause pain and injury to Donnie and me—which seemed contradictory. Next the legal team's hopes would rest on whether or not a jury would agree and then compensate us for our injuries and intentional violence that occurred as a result of the filmmakers' actions. In my opinion this made the whole damned thing a bum deal.

As the old saying goes: something is better than nothing. So after a lot of agonizing Greene and Quigley ultimately chose to settle the civil lawsuit in 2006, only days before the trial was to begin.

The result was that the defendants weren't punished at all.

Neither Donnie nor I would receive a lot of money from the settlement. After legal expenses that amount would be whittled down even more; in my case probably not a whole lot more than what Ryan had offered me in the first place. Since Donnie was still an alcoholic on the streets, he was assigned a court-appointed conservator to monitor and protect his share of the money.

Media reports greatly exaggerated what we received. People whom I knew from the VA, AA, and the VVSD would stop me on the street and high-five me, calling me a millionaire. I didn't have the heart to tell them the truth. I felt like I was representing all the other homeless guys who had also gotten screwed over in the videos, so I just smiled and went on my way.

———

The settlement put the public's mind at ease. They believed that justice had been done and the awful kids who had caused this had been appropriately punished. Besides, the public probably thought that since we were homeless, this was a huge amount of money for us. Many people seemed to picture us magically buying homes with picket fences, having wives, kids, dogs, and perfect lives. Many thought that lack of money had been the only reason we ended up in our situation in the first place. Now that our lawyers had "fixed" this, we had no excuse not to become "normal" again. It's amazing what people can say to themselves to get stuff that they'd rather not think about off their minds. But I could relate to this. After all, I'd been using alcohol for the same reason for at least forty years.

One thing I did know was that there remained a lot of work ahead of me, not only to create and maintain this "normal life," but also to help set things right where the court cases had left off. For me that meant doing everything I could to help make sure homeless people were protected against this violence ever happening again.

As the *Bumfights* cases played out on an international media stage, there were of course the expected reactions. Despite our status as unsympathetic victims, Donnie's and my situations caused the proper moral outrage. How could two defenseless men—veterans at that—be treated like this? What had the filmmakers been thinking? Didn't those kids have a conscience?

On the flip side, however, the more typical American sensationalism had also kicked into high gear. Prior to the criminal trial, radio shock jock Howard Stern had interviewed Ryan and his pals on his show. Listener reactions were mixed, but as usual Ryan attempted to smooth talk most concerns with his brand of manipulation and persuasion. To the surprise of many, Stern wasn't buying it. The shock jock showed sympathy for what Donnie and I had gone through and anger toward Ryan and the others. He christened me Rufus the Stunt Bum. This would subsequently stick in the marketing of the videos, as well as word of mouth. I know that wasn't what Stern had in mind.

Another terrible result of all the publicity—aside from increased video sales—was a series of copycat crimes that continue around the globe to this day. In Australia four teenagers killed a homeless man by burning him alive in his tent. Five teens in Alberta, Canada, beat a homeless guy with bottles and a club and then urinated on his face. A production company in England filmed its own version of the hit American videos. In Corpus Christi, Texas, two teenagers and a twenty-two-year-old man attacked a homeless guy from behind, kicking him to the ground while narrating the attack for a video camera. The list goes on and on, and I feel sick just thinking about all the violence now happening against the homeless, especially since they have no way of fighting back or anywhere to hide. It seemed obvious to me that the *Bumfights* videos had taken something that might have already been happening and made it a hundred times worse.

———

I talked about this and other things on my mind during a never-ending string of media interviews. It seemed as if every time I turned around, I was looking into a camera and talking to a reporter. From *The Abrams Report* and *The Today Show* to Greta Van Susteren, Court TV, and Geraldo Rivera on Fox, I patiently answered reporters' questions the best I could.

The undisputed highlight of our media junket was sitting down with veteran journalist Ed Bradley in 2006. But before that interview could happen, we had to find Donnie.

We were supposed to meet *60 Minutes* segment producer Michael Karzis at a grocery store near Barry Soper's townhouse complex at 1:00 p.m. on the day before the interview. Karzis had heard the media reports about *Bumfights* and also about the violence being perpetrated on homeless people. He had contacted Browne Greene's office, and everything was arranged through Kathy Pinckert, the law firm's director for marketing and media relations.

Karzis had checked us into an upscale hotel room for the night. This was mainly so he would know where to find us—meaning Donnie—for the interview the next morning. I arrived at the grocery store, but Donnie failed to show. Karzis and I drove around and looked for my friend.

"Michael, you know Donnie's going to look for something to drink as soon as we get to the room tonight," I said.

"That's not going to work. Don't let him drink," Karzis said. "And do me a favor: let him know that if he wants any food or *regular* drinks, just order them from room service. Don't leave the hotel."

"I'll do my best," I said, although I was dubious.

"I need you guys in good shape for tomorrow. I'm serious. If Donnie is drunk, you won't be able to participate in the show, and the *Bumfights* piece will be cut."

My heart sank. Karzis clearly had no idea what he was asking here. Trying to keep Donnie from drinking was something that many people had tried and failed to do, including me.

We eventually tracked him down on the other side of La Mesa. He stood outside a liquor store up the street from the Mobil gas station where we had first been attacked by the media after our escape from Las Vegas.

In the car Donnie whispered to me, "I gotta have a beer as soon as we get there."

I remembered this feeling. It was as if someone were stepping on the IV line carrying the drugs into your body that were the difference between life and death—or at the very least between a bearable life and a terrible state of suffering.

"Listen, Donnie, you don't have to go out and find a liquor store. All you have to do is order it on the phone from room service," I said.

Donnie's face lit up. "Really?" he asked.

"But you've gotta be straight for the interview by tomorrow. And don't you dare tell Michael I said it's okay to drink."

As soon as we checked into the Westin San Diego, Donnie grabbed the phone and ordered two beers from room service. I ordered dinner. When Donnie finished the two beers, he ordered two more. And so on...

"Donnie, if you're messed up tomorrow, they're just going to interview me," I warned him.

Donnie waved me off as he dialed the phone. He was calling his girlfriend, Linda—a woman not exactly playing with all her marbles, in my opinion—to let her know where he was staying.

"Yeah, come on down. Bring your friends," Donnie said.

I was pissed. I had visions of this ritzy hotel room turning into the E-Z 8, complete with crapping puppies and homeless guys in sleeping bags.

"If anyone shows up, you can get the hell out of here and meet them somewhere else!" I told Donnie.

"Oh relax, nobody's going to—"

The phone rang, and Donnie answered. I listened as he talked to one of Linda's friends. As Donnie gave her directions, I groaned. Not again. After he hung up, Donnie called room service and ordered another round.

"I really was hoping to straighten out some things with you tonight before the interview," I said.

But Donnie was pretty well drunk by now and just stared at me with glazed eyes. The next time the phone rang I grabbed for it, fearing that an entire harem of La Mesa women would be asking for directions to the hotel. But Barry was on the other end.

"You'd better get down here right away," I told him.

A short while later Barry stood frozen in the doorway, his jaw hanging in horror. Donnie sat on his bed in a sea of empty beer bottles while I sat on the other bed, tired and frustrated with my roommate. It had been easier living with Donnie when we were both drunk. To tell the truth now that I was sober and clearheaded, I found Donnie irritating.

Barry walked in, and I said, "What the hell can we do?"

"What's going on here, Donnie?" Barry asked.

"I got a girl comin' over; that's what the hell is goin' on," Donnie slurred, laughing in his face.

Adding insult to injury, the room-service guy rolled another cart full of beers into the room.

"Donnie, do you know how big this interview is tomorrow? What the hell are you doing? What's the matter with you!"

"Don't worry 'bout me. I'm good," Donnie said.

Luckily the women did not show up. And when Donnie woke up early the next morning, he seemed coherent. That is, until he spoke.

"I need a beer," he announced.

My heart sank, but I fought to stay optimistic. Michael Karzis and the limo would be there to pick us up in less than an hour.

Donnie had some light beers from the small refrigerator in the room and then got cleaned up. He wasn't drunk, but the beers were just enough to take the edge off and make him tolerable to be around. I was surprised that Donnie actually looked sober, especially considering his binge the night before.

In the limo on the way to a warehouse in Escondido, where the interview would take place, Michael Karzis discussed with us the details of our lives. When we walked into the warehouse basement—the quietest place for an interview, Karzis explained—I was startled by the number of crew people it took to film one guy interviewing two other guys. There were people setting up giant screens, lights on big metal stands, and a lot of other equipment. Barry was already there with his son, Blair, now an attorney and a public defender, Kathy Pinckert, and Mark Quigley. Karzis showed Donnie and me where we would be sitting and gave us an outline of what would be happening.

Finally Ed Bradley himself showed up. Now I didn't know who he was, but I quickly got an idea of his importance by everyone's respectful reaction when this tall, distinguished man stepped out of a limo. Ed spoke with us for a few minutes and gave us a rundown of the questions he would be asking. When the questions involved Ryan and the filmmakers, I could see how angry it made Ed. But when he talked to Donnie and me, it was as if we already knew one another. He even asked how we felt about some of the questions and the way the interview would go. I suddenly recalled the feelings groups at the VA hospital rehab program. Ed, I thought, was a real compassionate person and easy to talk to. I immediately felt comfortable around him, and the interview went smoothly. He didn't try to put us on the spot; we just had an easy conversation. I left the warehouse with a positive opinion of the longtime, highly respected journalist.

The *Bumfights* interview, which would air in October 2006, would be one of Ed Bradley's final *60 Minutes* assignments before he died a month later, on November 9. He left a great void that few could hope to fill. I'm proud that I had the chance to meet him.

During *60 Minutes* and all the rest of the interviews, I was able to reveal various details of my life, some that I had almost forgotten. I covered a wide range of topics with the reporters. Along with Donnie, I was an object of fascination for the press. They wanted to know about being homeless, the *Bumfights* stunts, of course, about my drinking, and everything else they figured would interest the American public. Individual reporters' faces became a blur, and I only remember bits and pieces of the interviews.

"How do you feel most Americans think about homeless people like you and Donnie?" one reporter said.

"Most people probably think that all homeless people are lazy, that they don't want to work and are on drugs and alcohol. In reality, probably about 30 percent are alcoholics or addicts."

The reporter acted surprised at how well spoken I was on the subject of homelessness. That made me smile.

In another interview I said, "We need to be doing something about homelessness in America. With all the money we spend on war, we should be able to find a way for people to afford housing. I don't see why people are homeless and hungry in America, because this is supposed to be a rich country."

I added, "I saw so much food wasted when I lived behind a grocery store. They would bring out tons of day-old bread and pastries every morning, and all the rich folks would drive up in their BMWs and load up their trunks."

As I told them stories of what I had observed on the street—the eyes and ears of society—one reporter asked the inevitable question: "What do you want people to do, Rufus? What do you want to come from all this?"

"Well, one thing I thought of is if more homeless people were registered to vote, their voices could finally be heard. It would make a great deal of difference. If our governor knew that five thousand to ten thousand homeless people were registered voters, he'd have to do something."

"What can our viewers do?"

"I want them to write to Congress or their governor and say, 'I want to see more homeless registered to vote,'" I said. "In fact you can let people know that I plan to start a voter-registration drive at the Operation Stand Down event in San Diego to get homeless people to vote. Most of them are veterans who fought for our country so we can be free. I figure they should have some say in who we elect to lead it."

This was a sentiment that I quickly put into motion by registering to vote at the San Diego County registrar's office.

And of course, on that note, the topic of alcohol always had to be brought up. It was at the core of almost everything bad that had happened in my life.

"How are you doing now with your sobriety?" just about every reporter asked.

"My life is good today."

"Why is that, Rufus?"

"I'm not drinking," I said.

"Why did you stop?"

"Because it was killing me."

I had found the time to reflect on this, even in between the stress of going to court and to deposition hearings and squinting at the glare of camera lights. I'd miraculously escaped death at birth from an addiction to the bottle that was beyond my control. Now I had done the same from an addiction that was entirely my responsibility. Fortunately this time my recovery and my future were also entirely my responsibility. I had been given a new shot at life, and I vowed to make the best of it—to do what I could for as many homeless men and women as possible and to stay sober forever.

CHAPTER 15

REBIRTH

I SUCCESSFULLY PLUGGED ALONG ON MY ROAD TO RECOVERY.
My head had cleared up so much after the first couple of years of
sobriety that by 2004 I decided I really wanted to give back to the
community, specifically to an organization that gave back to veterans.

The program was called Operation Stand Down—a big, successful
nonprofit organization in San Diego that provides annual programs
to assist homeless veterans. I volunteered for its three-day weekend
program, during which a local high school field turns into a military base
to help veterans. I'd learned from the VA and VVSD how well-known
among veterans Operation Stand Down was for providing everything
from showers, a clean change of clothes, and toiletries to social worker,
legal, and psychiatric services—basically, anything the vets needed.

Since the media continued to be fascinated with my *Bumfights*
adventures, they tracked me down at the event. I allowed myself to
be interviewed for the front page of the local section in San Diego's
main newspaper. Yeah, I wanted to promote Operation Stand Down
and its services, but I also had another motive. I'd been thinking a lot
about Donnie and wanted to find him. I talked about my best friend
throughout the article and how much I was worried about him, with

the hope that Donnie would read the story and decide to reenter the program. Sure, it was a long shot, but it was the only shot I had at the moment.

However, before Donnie ever saw the article, Barry found him on the streets of La Mesa. Donnie was drunk, of course. Barry eventually managed to convince him to give the VVSD program a try. But Donnie once again failed, probably for the same reasons that I figured had made him fail the first time. Once more Donnie went in the opposite direction from me as I continued to work hard to remain in my new life of sobriety.

While Donnie went backward, I went steadily forward, soon moving into a sober-living complex in Escondido called New Resolve. For me this seemed like the perfect phrase to describe my life.

The therapy I received at New Resolve helped me to talk more about things. I even managed to discuss all those darn feelings, something that always frustrated me at the VA. I had never felt real emotions on the streets. Sure, I still needed a therapist to explain exactly what feelings were, but this was definitely a better start.

New Resolve represented a big turning point in my life. I found a new job along with my new lease on life—and a lease on an apartment in nearby Oceanside. A friend of Barry's owned the complex— and soon after leaving New Resolve I took a lease on an apartment in nearby Oceanside. I had saved a little money while working and living at New Resolve, and I used some of it for the down payment, rent, and security deposit on my new place.

Barry took me shopping in a borrowed pickup truck for furniture, linens, appliances, and other things that I hadn't owned since I was a young guy back in the South. I was floored by the five-hundred-dollar price tag I saw on a bed. A *bed*—something that, before the rehab beds, I hadn't known for over fifteen years. Heck, I would've been content to toss a sleeping bag on the floor, but Barry laughed and told me, "Rufus, you *need* a bed." I thought of Donnie, sleeping on the streets somewhere in La Mesa, and knew how true that statement was.

As the shopping trip continued, so did my sense of being in some kind of weird dream. A microwave for $169! This made me wonder what the stove was for.

"I ain't paying ten dollars for no pillowcase," I firmly told Barry at one point.

I soon got into a daily routine. Since my eyesight was too poor to drive, I would wake up at four every morning, catch the bus from Oceanside to the train station just after five, and board a train to San Diego to work for Barry. The commute took two and a half hours each way. And every evening, like clockwork, I would attend an AA meeting, shower, and then go to bed. I continued that schedule for a year, until I finally rented a studio apartment five minutes from my construction job at Lakewood Villa, Barry's townhouse complex, where we had first met.

As for my best friend, I knew in my heart that when Donnie chose to give up on the possibility of sobriety, he was also giving up on our friendship. I saw him every once in a while on the streets of La Mesa, along with my other homeless friends. But every time I left Donnie, I felt like I was saying good-bye for the last time.

After one such weekend visit with Donnie—I had tracked him down to a familiar spot outside the library—I returned home. I sighed as I dropped my keys onto the kitchen table and looked around. It wasn't a huge place, but it was all mine. I sat down on the couch and turned on the used television I'd gotten from the VVSD. (As it turned out, I could have gotten all the things I'd bought for free or real cheap at the VVSD.) I thought about how most guys would crack open a cold beer and watch the evening sports scores. I wondered if Barry's Red Sox had played that day. I wondered what else I was supposed to be thinking about now that I was finally a normal, blue-collar, working-class citizen again.

But what I mostly thought about was my best friend, Donnie. He had really looked like shit that day. Drunker than ever, he continued to date a woman who seemed to have a ton of emotional problems and was just encouraging him to be worse. Or maybe she was making him look good so that he could keep denying that his life was as bad as it was. I had recently figured out why Donnie was so hostile toward me these days. When we were together on the streets, I was always drunker, always more pissed off, and always in more trouble than he. This allowed Donnie to be the charmer, our spokesperson, you could say. As long as I was farther down in the sewer than he, Donnie's life was in balance. And now that I was okay, Donnie had no use for me anymore. Something I could never have imagined before was now crystal clear.

—-—

I liked working for Barry and earning a living. But in the midst of all my successes during my recovery, there were a few experiences that really excited me. The first was my work in helping the other homeless vets at Operation Stand Down. More and more, I thought about my self-worth. I felt like I was on the verge of some great opportunities to help other folks, especially those in positions that I had once found myself: homeless veterans. Since I had walked a hell of a lot longer than a mile in their shoes, I felt like I knew exactly what was needed to help them. Next I wanted to make sure that what happened to Donnie and me in the *Bumfights* videos never happened to another homeless person again. I made a mental note to talk to Barry about these issues. Barry could usually come up with the right name and phone number for anything I needed. I swear the guy was a walking information directory.

And finally I remembered how much I enjoyed those large-print books Barry had brought me at the VA hospital. I learned a lot of new words that way, and the idea of additional learning excited me. I also figured that if I was going to really help my fellow homeless vets as best as I could, I would need to build up my education.

So I decided to go back to school and pick up where I had left off many years ago. Thanks to some help from the Disabled American Veterans Resource Center, this became a reality. I enrolled at Palomar College, a community college. I didn't have any specific career goals, but I did have a general idea of what I wanted to learn: math, computers, and engineering, among other things.

My new love of reading continued in my college English class. I worked on my new language skills with a lot of writing assignments.

Throughout my college experience, my aim was to do well and never settle for being a B student. I had some free time on the weekends, and I devoted it all to studying. This hard work paid off, and I earned a 3.6 grade point average during the first semester.

The continuing *Bumfights* court cases, however, soon messed with my schedule. I couldn't immediately go back to school, but I figured that would eventually change. I knew that once I set my mind to doing something, I wouldn't allow anything to get in the way. After my first semester I thought hard about studying sociology. I figured that I might enjoy a branch of science devoted to the study of people, especially why people do the crazy things they do. Hell, I'd had a lifetime of experience with that.

By 2005 homelessness, *Bumfights*, and alcoholism were three years behind me. Yet somehow the story of the *Bumfights* kept following me around. Many people recognized me from the videos, and some shouted, "Hey, Rufus the Stunt Bum! We love you, man!" This was always humiliating to me.

Then one day something completely unexpected happened. I heard that Ryan McPherson and Zachary Bubeck were back in court with their attorneys, asking the judge to release them from their probation because they had complied with the mandatory order of working for 280 hours at a homeless shelter. Deputy DA Curtis Ross advised the judge that the document stating that McPherson and Bubeck had completed the hours was a phony. It had not been signed by an official, but forged—unbelievably—by a homeless person. The judge temporarily denied McPherson and Bubeck's motion. In 2006 a whole new case unfolded.

True to form those two punks had never for a minute believed that they'd done anything wrong and therefore did not think they should be punished for anything. It pissed me off when I heard that they had found a homeless man to sign the papers for them. I couldn't believe that, after all this, those assholes still hadn't learned their lesson.

I was relieved to hear that the pair were later sentenced to six months in jail for the forgery and for violating the terms of their probation. But rather than doing any jail time, they served their time at a work camp. I thought that was a damned light sentence, considering the crimes they had committed. But some punishment was better than none, I guess. Finally a small bit of justice.

While I was glad to hear that Ryan and Zachary had finally gotten some punishment, oddly it didn't affect me as much anymore. These days I preferred to focus on the positive instead. Those guys were bad seeds, and they probably would never change. I might not be able to do anything about that, but I could do a lot of things to help protect the homeless, give them a voice, and maybe prevent other kids from thinking that beating up innocent people was somehow fun and harmless.

Barry and I had talked about this, and he arranged for me to meet Michael Stoops, the chairman of the National Coalition for the Homeless. Our meeting took place in San Diego, and we hit it off like old friends. We discussed the most important issues facing homeless people, mainly the news stories about kids beating up on them. Michael recruited me to speak to students at universities all across the United States and to share my experiences.

Starting in the spring of 2006, through the coalition's Faces of Homelessness Speakers' Bureau, I spoke on panels with other previously homeless people at universities all across the country. In the course of one year I traveled to a long list of schools, among them UCLA, USC, Azusa Pacific University, Seattle Pacific University, the University of Montana, Manhattan College, the University of San Diego, the University of Wisconsin, and Syracuse University. The panel was always diverse: me, a recovering alcoholic; a woman who had been a victim of domestic violence; someone with schizophrenia; another with bipolar disorder; and so on.

I began my speeches by talking about my life growing up, how I was raised with alcohol as a medicine. I would talk about my marriages, my kids, becoming homeless, and all the other personal details. Most of the students were interested in what my life was like now: whether

I was in touch with my kids, if I was working, and my experiences of speaking at other universities.

These speeches truly made me feel like I had a mission. I felt like a teacher, and I wanted to teach these young people about how precious life is, as well as the challenges of being homeless. I emphasized the choices that we all make and how those choices influence who and what we are and who we become.

At the California State University, San Bernardino, Professor Brian Levin, another friend of Barry's, got everyone's attention with some startling statistics about homelessness and violence against the homeless. I remember listening as Brian reeled off the facts: "There are approximately 754,000 unsheltered homeless in America and 334,744 living in emergency or transient shelters. In a 2001 California study, 66 percent of homeless who were surveyed reported being criminally victimized; 75 percent of the victims reported being assaulted."

I watched the young faces in the crowd as Brian spoke and also when those of us on the panel took turns telling our own heartbreaking stories. I saw the effect the panel was having on them: mostly shock, some awe, and sadness.

I figured that some of the kids knew who I was. The *Bumfights* videos and DVDs were popular in college dorms. And now, with the Internet and video-downloading websites like YouTube, Rufus the Stunt Bum had become the stuff of college-guy folklore. I was even the subject of drinking games they'd play while they watched the videos: "Do a shot every time Rufus falls down."

But a strange thing happened once I started to speak in a sober, personable voice about my life story and the events that led me to take part in those terrible videos years earlier. The same kids who had laughed at me and cheered me on in the videos now felt guilty for having done so. The students in the audience watched and listened to me, an extremely human, remorseful, imperfect man standing before them. They saw me tear up when I talked about how much I regretted the effect that my actions had on my wives, children, and others in my family. They watched me get angry at myself and at the *Bumfights* filmmakers. And they heard the sadness and concern in my voice as I talked about my best friend, Donnie, who still lived on the streets. This was not a warm and fuzzy goodwill speaking tour, but instead a reality check for anyone who thought they knew what homelessness was and understood what would make a man get so drunk, climb into a shopping cart, and allow himself to be pushed down a flight of concrete steps.

The experiences weren't always great, though. Once, our panel spoke at a continuation school for troubled teenagers in Maryland. I remember how the auditorium was filled with leather-jacketed kids with nose rings and spikes through their faces. As the event neared an end, one of the leather-clad kids stood up and raised his hand. Michael Stoops called on him.

"I just wanted to say to Rufus that you're my hero," the kid said, smirking.

I had a bad feeling about that smirk. The kid reminded me of Ryan.

"Yeah, why's that?" I asked him.

"Because of all the stuff you did in the videos. That was cool." The kid laughed and sat down.

This reminded me of an experience I'd had while working at Barry's townhouse complex. A woman, her son, and his friends approached. They'd recognized me from the *Bumfights* videos; they were apparently big fans. They took pictures with me while showing special interest in the damned tattoos on my knuckles. And like that troubled high school kid in Maryland, they told me how I was their hero—for all the wrong reasons, of course.

Fortunately the positive experiences are far more common. At Azusa Pacific in California, after I had finished talking about the impact of *Bumfights* on my life, a young man stood and raised his hand. At first I was worried it would be a rerun of the smirking punk from the Maryland high school. But then I saw that the kid had tears in his eyes.

"I-I just wanted to say," he stammered, "that me and my friends watched the *Bumfights* videos in high school. We used to laugh and drink and have a good time…"

The kid's voice trailed off as he tried to compose himself. I said, "Don't worry about it, man."

"No. I just need to say that I'm really sorry, man."

I smiled. "Thanks. I appreciate that."

Mission accomplished. Sure, this was hard work, and you always ran the risk of an inappropriate response. But breakthroughs like this, which could change a life, made it all worthwhile.

———

During Michael Stoops's visit in 2006, I did a training film for POST (California Commission on Peace Officers Standards and Training). I was uniquely qualified, I guess, to help educate police officers about how best to deal with homeless people humanely, intelligently, and safely. The homeless were, as I had always thought, like owls in the night, the unpaid eyes and ears of the police. The name of the film was *Law Enforcement Response to Homelessness*, a telecourse for police officers. The program was delivered to hundreds of POST law-enforcement agencies throughout California.

Just before the POST videotaping, I addressed a seminar attended by law-enforcement officers, district attorneys, and members of the attorney general's office. I spoke about my experiences as a homeless person and then took questions for forty-five minutes. Afterward these people—who would go on to teach others how to interact with the homeless—approached me to offer their appreciation.

One of Michael's and my ultimate objectives, however, was on a larger scale. We wanted to make assaults on the homeless an official hate crime, and therefore a felony with greater penalties. This was probably the most ambitious goal I had ever worked toward in my life. I became more committed to this than I had ever been to anything in my life. On some crazy level, I felt that succeeding in this would start to make up for all the relationships, marriages, and jobs I had failed at so miserably in the past.

I thought of the physical pain, the humiliation, and most of all how I felt when sitting in the courtroom watching the *Bumfights* filmmakers get off with so little punishment. I was determined to turn the bum deal that Donnie and I received into something positive that would aid—and hopefully save the lives of—many helpless people across the country.

Early in 2006 another friend of Barry's stepped forward to help me. When San Diego County District Attorney Bonnie Dumanis heard the story of the *Bumfights*, and more important, the story of how far I had come from homelessness and hopelessness to humanitarian, she wrote a letter to California State Senator Christine Kehoe. Together the two prepared legislation called the Rufus Hannah Act. It emphasized that any violent act against a homeless person would mandate an additional three years in sentencing. The only problem was that it was June when the bill was ready for submission, which was too late to get the legislation successfully "into the hopper," as it was commonly known in politics. The lawmakers would have to wait until early 2007, regroup, and try again. Through a lucky coincidence, though, I wouldn't have to wait that long.

The *60 Minutes* interview aired in October 2006. State Senator Darrell Steinberg happened to be watching that night. Steinberg was already a vocal advocate for the homeless, and he took action immediately. He proposed legislation, designated SB 122, similar to what Senator Kehoe had tried to introduce unsuccessfully. The legislation once again didn't pass in January 2007, but Steinberg planned to reintroduce SB 122 in January 2008 and every subsequent January, if that's what it took to get the bill passed. All the people who were suddenly on my side humbled me, especially after all those years when no one had had my back.

Well, I guess *one* person had my back. Without Barry Soper, I would not be here to tell this story. I have no doubt about that. Yes, he is my employer, but I never think of him like that. He is my *friend.* We'd come a long way from mistrusting—shoot, even disliking—each other. It had taken me a long time to appreciate Barry's heartfelt assistance and kindness. And I couldn't blame him if he had ever thought that he was wasting his time on me. But I'm so glad he never gave up on me.

———

During the summer of 2007, to Barry's surprise, he received a phone call from Bill Hannah, my brother. Bill, also a recovering alcoholic, now lived in San Mateo, California. Barry helped put him in touch with me, and the two of us arranged a visit.

On the day that I opened the door of my La Mesa apartment, I welcomed my guest with a big grin. The man standing there was a little taller and a good deal older. A gray beard and mustache covered much of his face now. But that was to be expected. After all, it had been seventeen years since I'd last seen Bill. He was surely a sight for sore eyes.

"It's nice to see you again, Billy," I told my brother.

Bill reached out and started to shake my hand, but then he pulled me into a big bear hug. "You too, Rufus," he said.

I led the way over to the couch. For a moment we just sat there, looking at each other.

"Can I get you something to drink?" I asked.

"Got any beer?" Bill asked.

"You're kidding, right?"

Billy cracked the same wiseass smile I remembered. "Yeah, of course I am. Just thought I'd put you to the test, Brother."

"Did you have any trouble getting here?" I asked.

"Nah. Your directions were good." He looked around the little apartment. "Nice place."

"Thanks."

As we caught up on old times, I couldn't help but replay in my mind the last time I had seen my brother. I was drunk and on the brink of becoming homeless. Within a year I'd left on a cross-country van journey with a guy named Tim and two women. I wondered what would have happened if Bill and I had worked out our differences that night. If I'd never left for San Diego, never met Donnie—never encountered Ryan McPherson—where would we be standing today?

Bill seemed to be thinking the same thing.

"I'm just really surprised at what's happened to you," Bill said. "Especially considering...you know."

"So you already knew about the videos and all that?" I asked. Back then I'd never even thought about how my family might react to hearing about *Bumfights*—or worse, how they would react if they had actually seen the videos.

"Yeah, Jenny had filled me in. The worst part was that we didn't know where you were or how to find you."

"Sorry. I was thinking about you guys a lot," I said, and I really meant it.

"Yeah. That must have been rough," Bill said.

"It was. But I had a lot to do with it. It wasn't just bad luck, you know." That was for damned sure. Taking responsibility for my actions felt good.

"I know. And I'm really proud of how you pulled yourself out of this."

I nodded. "I had a lot of help. And when it came down to it, I didn't want to die. Not like that anyway, drunk and on the streets."

"Well, the whole family's real proud of you now."

I stared at him intently. "They talk about me?"

"Of course we do. You were all over the news there for a while. What choice did we have?" Bill laughed.

Now I shifted uncomfortably in my seat, and my face got red. I hated thinking about that time.

"What, suddenly you're embarrassed for getting your life back together? Everyone back home is saying how strong you turned out to be able to do all this."

"Strong? I never thought of it like that." I shook my head.

"Yeah, well, that's how I see it. It took a lot of strength to go through this and come out even better than you were before."

"That wouldn't take much. Especially compared to the last time you saw me."

I felt like the subject had to come up eventually, so it might as well be now.

"Yeah, you were definitely shit-faced that night when you came home," Bill said. "And you were being a complete ass, and I got pissed. I finally said to myself, screw it, he's got to learn to take care of himself sooner or later, so it might as well be now."

"So that's why you kicked me out? To make me stronger?" Maybe he was wiser than I'd ever given him credit for. But of course I couldn't have seen it then.

"Yes. And I felt guilty afterward, for a long time—especially when Jenny updated me on what was happening to you, starting with when you were homeless in San Diego. I felt like it was all my fault."

"It wasn't," I assured him.

Bill paused.

"Yeah, I know that now. It took me a while, though. But then I started reading about all the great stuff you've been doing to help the homeless. Maybe that kick in the ass was good for you, brother." He smiled.

"Yeah, I probably needed it—and deserved it too," I said.

Bill slapped me on the shoulder and laughed. "You were something back then; that's for sure."

"I was *nothing*, actually. Worthless to pretty much everyone in my life—including you," I said.

Bill shook his head. "I don't think a person can be totally worthless."

"I still wonder what it would be like if none of that stuff had happened."

"I honestly don't think that was the plan," Bill said.

I frowned, not convinced.

"Don't you see, Rufus? All this had to happen so you could be reborn the person you are today."

Reborn. That was a good word to use, because reborn was exactly how I felt. Having Bill here now reminded me that I had come full circle. The day he'd kicked me out had been the last day that I'd seen a member of my family, the last day before all those years of homelessness. Now he was back.

Man, this felt so good. I suddenly wrapped Bill up in a huge bear hug and didn't let go for a while. Bill might have been uncomfortable about all the attention from his big brother.

I didn't care.

CHAPTER 16

From HOPELESS *to* HUMANITARIAN

In January 2008 Barry and I traveled to Sacramento with Brian Levin. There, I would be presented with the California Association of Human Relations Organizations (CAHRO) Civil Rights Award.

Levin, also the director of the Center for the Study of Hate and Extremism at California State, San Bernardino, had nominated me for the award. Part of the mission of CAHRO is to promote acceptance of all people through activities that protect human and civil rights. The award is presented at a luncheon at the Embassy Suites Hotel in Sacramento as a part of the day's conference, which also includes a number of panel discussions.

I sat at my table studying the program and reading the bios of the nine other distinguished recipients on the program, trying to see where in the heck I fit in.

"You ready, Rufus?" Levin asked.

"I guess so," I answered nervously, feeling the weight of responsibility.

Brian smiled encouragingly and walked up to the front of the large room. CAHRO's president, Robin Toma, came to the microphone and talked about the award that the others and I would be receiving.

"These Californians have demonstrated a commitment to civil rights and human relations and have exemplified a commitment to civil rights and human relations in their life and in their work," he said. Toma then introduced Brian Levin, who in turn introduced me.

Up until a few years ago, most people knew of him as Rufus the Stunt Bum in a series of videotapes called Bumfights, *which were sold on the Internet. The videos depicted homeless people, drunk or high on drugs, assaulting one another and taking part in dangerous and even life-endangering stunts. That was how Rufus was known more than five years ago—as an inebriated homeless man who would do anything for a beer. Rufus was not unlike Job in the Bible, with one bad circumstance following another: unemployment, divorce, disability, homelessness, and then the life-threatening injuries that came with the* Bumfights. *But since those dark times, Rufus has fought back and brought his life into the light, become and remained sober, restored the bonds of family, gone back to college after dropping out of high school, remained steadily employed, and assisted thousands of homeless veterans in registering to vote. Today we are recognizing Rufus for the outstanding contributions he has made to the California community in the area of human rights. A few years ago Rufus Hannah was a man who had nothing. He turned his life around through sheer will and righteousness and decided to help others. Rufus went from the lowest level of human despair and misery to becoming a human being recognized for greatness. If someone like him can make this kind of impact and positive change, what a wonderful, inspiring lesson it is for the rest of us, who have so much more in our lives. Ladies and gentlemen, distinguished guests: Mr. Rufus Hannah.*

Amid loud applause, "Mr." Rufus Hannah stepped up to the podium and thanked everyone I could think of for this honor. Then I said how I hoped to use this kind of recognition as an opportunity to create positive change for homeless people. People cringed when I talked about the violence of the *Bumfights* stunts. They were choked up along with me when I talked about my regrets (injuring Donnie and failing my wives, my kids, and myself). And they smiled at my triumphs. They seemed pleasantly surprised when I announced my current successes: speaking at colleges and universities, going back to school, and fighting for hate-crime legislation that would protect the homeless.

Another burst of applause surprised me when I announced plans to see an earlier dream come to fruition by giving potentially thousands of homeless veterans a voice for change by registering them to vote at the July 2008 Operation Stand Down event in San Diego, the first-ever program of its kind in California. The program was finally becoming a reality with the help of the California registrar of voters, as well as Michael Stoops and Darcy Pavich, Operation Stand Down coordinator, and her husband, Al, CEO of the VVSD. I announced how we'd already made plans to take this voter-registration program to homeless shelters all over California and eventually to other major cities across America. I had clear reasons for giving as many homeless people as possible a voice in their government and therefore their own lives.

"I want the politicians to recognize that violence against the homeless must stop, and I hope that programs like this will eventually assist in ending homelessness in America," I said.

Brian motioned for me to wrap up the speech. I didn't have anything else scribbled on the back of the program, so I simply closed from the heart.

My first time being born was a shaky situation—I almost didn't make it. My parents didn't always make the best choices, but they always loved me and my brother and sister, no matter what. Many years later I was born again after almost dying from drinking and from making bad decisions while I was drinking. This whole experience has shown me that I'm capable of doing just about anything I put my mind to. And for that I am grateful and thankful to God every single day. So if I had to do it again, I'd still be born in Swainsboro, Georgia, the same way I was the first time to the same family of loving people. I'd just be real careful next time to never stop believing that I have a right to live a good life. A life where I don't let anyone tell me that I'm not worth much more than a beer. A life where I can fall asleep every night and wake up every morning and feel safe. I think everyone deserves a shot at that, don't you? Thank you very much.

I received another round of thunderous applause, which turned into a standing ovation. This applause touched me the most. It scared me a bit too. I held back the urge to run off and hide. I then recalled when I first came to understand what applause really meant.

I was six years old, and the family lived in our original home in Swainsboro. Everyone was listening to the *Grand Ole Opry* broadcast, and the kids were being quiet as usual. I sat cross-legged on the floor, squeezed between the recliner and the table with the radio on it. I could hear everything happening in the music hall as if I were right there, sitting in the front row. Tonight Loretta Lynn was performing, so I was particularly excited. Not because I was a big fan or anything, although I thought she had a pretty voice, but because of how much the people loved her.

Now it was coming up on my favorite part—she was about to finish the song. I cocked my head eagerly toward the radio, waiting. And then it came: the thunder of applause and cheering so loud that I thought the radio would break. My mom noticed the wide grin on my face.

"That must be something else," she said.

"Why do the people clap that hard for her?" I asked her.

"Because when you do something nice for a lot of people at once, they applaud to show their appreciation," my mother answered.

"They must *really* appreciate her," I said in awe.

Standing at the podium in Sacramento, I blinked back tears and smiled in appreciation and awe at the roomful of people applauding me. This had been a long, hard journey, and I'd wound up in a place that I could never have imagined. I plan on staying strong and working hard and never going back to that dark place again.

And the only way to do that is to keep in my heart that this is not the end of my journey. It is only the beginning.

The End

AFTERWORD

I AM NOW FIFTY-FIVE YEARS OLD, AND I CELEBRATED SEVEN YEARS of sobriety in October 2009. I continue to work full-time for Barry Soper, serving as assistant manager at Lakewood Villa Townhomes in San Diego—the same complex where Barry found me Dumpster diving in 1999. Every year since 2004 I have volunteered at San Diego's Operation Stand Down. At this event hundreds of homeless veterans are provided with a wide range of necessities, including food, clothing, medical, legal, and mental health assistance, job counseling and referral, companionship, and camaraderie. Operation Stand Down is a time for the community to connect with the homeless veteran population and address this crisis that affects every town, city, and state in this country.

I still serve on the Speakers' Bureau of the National Coalition for the Homeless. The Speakers' Bureau visits three hundred universities, colleges, high schools, and other venues each year, addressing approximately 140,000 people. I also continue to promote legislation aimed at making the abuse of homeless people a hate crime, thus imposing greater penalties on the perpetrators.

I try to remain modest when folks ask me about my recovery and the humanitarian work. What I believe in is "paying it forward." I want to do good things for others because others have done good things for me.

I now talk regularly with my two oldest children, Stephanie and Rufus III. In July 2008 I flew to North Carolina to see Rufus III and his family, and in September I returned to my hometown of Swainsboro, Georgia, to see Stephanie and her family. This was the first time I had seen any of them since they were young children. I also stay in touch with my brother, Bill, my sister, Jenny, and my aunt Dorothy. Both Stephanie and Rufus III have expressed interest in meeting my other children.

Being on the streets for as long as I was, I feel that I have a unique insight into people. I plan on going back to college to earn a degree in sociology.

———

Donnie Brennan, now sixty years old, continues to be haunted by his memories of Vietnam, like so many other veterans. He has undertaken rehab on three separate occasions, each one unsuccessful. His reply when asked why he is unable to complete a rehab: "I like to drink."

I have not seen Donnie Brennan for a long time. I'm sad about the fact that he has not changed, and it hurts me to see him as he still is.

But Donnie is at least off the streets. He lives in a trailer with his girlfriend, Linda, in Flinn Springs, an unincorporated area in the eastern part of San Diego County. Unemployed—and unemployable—he lives on his disability checks as well as the proceeds from the *Bumfights* civil suit settlement. A court-appointed conservator controls his finances and gives him an allowance. His mother, Virginia, still lives in La Mesa, and Donnie sees her occasionally.

—

Ryan McPherson, now twenty-six, continues to run Indecline Productions in Las Vegas. Among their documentary productions are *Assault: The World's Most Violent Collection of Real Street Fights*, *Blingalong: It's Worse Than You Think*, and a film described as "a fifteen-minute dry hump porno," *King of the Jews*.

McPherson, in a 2006 interview, states that, technically, he and his friends never made any money off the sales of *Bumfights*. Who knows what that meant? Sure, he might have spent a lot of money on defense attorneys, but trust me, the videos earned plenty of money.

When asked about me, he said, "In a way, the *Bumfights* video saved his life. During all of the legal bullshit, one of [his children] called and expressed her disappointment after seeing her father run his head into walls and fall down hills. He straightened up shortly thereafter."

—

Violence against the homeless continues across the country. The National Coalition for the Homeless published NCH Fact Sheet 21 in August 2007. Citing records kept from 1999 to 2006 and based on reports from advocates and homeless-shelter workers, the fact sheet mentions incidents of homeless men, women, and even children being harassed, kicked, set on fire, beaten to death, and even decapitated. During this period, 614 acts of violence were reported, resulting in 189 murders of homeless people. Twenty deaths occurred in 2006.

According to the fact sheet, most hate crimes and violent acts are committed not by organized hate groups, but by individuals who harbor a strong resentment against a certain group of people. Some are "mission offenders" who believe they are on a mission to cleanse the world of a particular evil. Others are "scapegoat offenders" who violently act out their resentment toward the perceived growing economic power of a particular racial or ethnic group. Still others are "thrill seekers," those who take advantage of a vulnerable and disadvantaged group in order to satisfy their own pleasures.

Thrill seekers, primarily in their teens, are the most common perpetrators of violence against people who are homeless. And these "thrill seekers, primarily in their teens," comprise the target audience for violence-laden videos such as *Bumfights* and its sequels.

ABOUT *the* AUTHORS

ACTIVIST AND HUMANITARIAN RUFUS HANNAH WORKS WITH the National Coalition for the Homeless Speakers' Bureau, where he visits colleges, universities, and high schools across the country, speaking out against violence to the homeless and educating people about homelessness. He has worked on hate-crime legislation with California State Senator Darrell Steinberg, the sponsor of Assembly Bill 2521. Hannah assisted the California Commission on Peace Officers Standards and Training (POST) in the making of a training film on how law-enforcement personnel can work better in dealing with the homeless population.

An alcoholic for nearly four decades and homeless for fifteen years, Hannah has been sober since 2002. Early in his recovery he began working with Operation Stand Down, a veterans organization that assists homeless veterans in the San Diego area. An army vet himself, he initiated a voter-registration drive for homeless veterans.

Born in Swainsboro, Georgia, Hannah received his GED diploma at the age of eighteen and has since resumed his education at Palomar College in the San Diego area. He continues to work for Barry Soper as assistant manager at Lakewood Villa Townhomes, where they first met in 1999 under "unique" circumstances.

Businessman Barry M. Soper is chairman of the board of Oak Grove, a nonprofit educational and residential treatment center serving 160 children, ages five to eighteen. Oak Grove, headquartered in Murrieta, California, provides twenty-four-hour care at its three campus dormitories for many of these children, the majority of whom have suffered physical or sexual abuse, neglect, or serious family conflicts. Its mission: "To rebuild the lives of at-risk children and their families through education, healing, restoring relationships, building character, and instilling hope."

Soper also owns and manages a number of apartment and townhouse properties in and around San Diego, including Lakewood Villa Townhomes, where he currently employs Rufus Hannah (formerly Rufus the Stunt Bum) as assistant manager.

Born in Worcester, Massachusetts, Soper graduated from the University of Bridgeport (CT) with a bachelor's degree in sociology. He attended law school on the West Coast but chose the business world over a career in law.

Soper has served on the board of St. Vincent de Paul Village. A key center for San Diego's large homeless population, St. Vincent de Paul's mission is to help its neighbors in need to break the cycle of homelessness and poverty by promoting self-sufficiency through an innovative continuum of care, multidisciplinary programs, and other partnerships. Soper has also served on the board of the San Diego Repertory Theatre.